Edited by Naomi Starkey

May–August 2009

Suggestions for using *New Daylight*

Find a regular time and place, if possible, where you can read and pray undisturbed. Before you begin, take time to be still and perhaps use the BRF prayer. Then read the Bible passage slowly (try reading it aloud if you find it over-familiar), followed by the comment. You can also use *New Daylight* for group study and discussion, if you prefer.

The prayer or point for reflection can be a starting point for your own meditation and prayer. Many people like to keep a journal to record their thoughts about a Bible passage and items for prayer. In *New Daylight* we also note the Sundays and some special festivals from the Church calendar, to keep in step with the Christian year.

New Daylight and the Bible

New Daylight contributors use a range of Bible versions, and you will find a list of the versions used in each issue at the back of the notes on page 154. You are welcome to use your own preferred version alongside the passage printed in the notes, and this can be particularly helpful if the Bible text has been abridged.

New Daylight affirms that the whole of the Bible is God's revelation to us, and we should read, reflect on and learn from every part of both Old and New Testaments. Usually the printed comment presents a straight-forward 'thought for the day', but sometimes it may also raise questions rather than simply providing answers, as we wrestle with some of the more difficult passages of Scripture.

New Daylight *is also available in a deluxe edition (larger format). Check out your local Christian bookshop or contact the BRF office, who can also give more details about a cassette version for the visually impaired. For a Braille edition, contact St John's Guild, 8 St Raphael's Court, Avenue Road, St Albans, AL1 3EH.*

Writers in this issue

Amy Boucher Pye is an American who has lived in the UK for over a decade. She makes her home in North London with her husband and young family and enjoys writing for Christian periodicals, including *Quiet Spaces*, *Woman Alive* and *Christian Marketplace*.

Naomi Starkey is the Editor of *New Daylight*. She also edits *Quiet Spaces*, BRF's prayer and spirituality journal, as well as commissioning BRF's range of books for adults. She has written *Good Enough Mother* for BRF.

Lisa Cherrett is BRF's Project Editor and Managing Editor for the Bible reading notes. She serves as a member of the leadership team in her local Baptist church.

John Proctor works for the United Reformed Church, teaching the New Testament in Cambridge and around the church. John has written *The People's Bible Commentary: Matthew* (BRF, 2001) and booklets on the Gospels in the Grove Biblical Series.

Gordon Giles is a vicar in Enfield, north-west London, previously based at St Paul's Cathedral, where his work involved musical and liturgical responsibilities. He is trained in music, philosophy and theology.

David Robertson has ministered in a variety of parishes since his ordination in 1979 and is currently a vicar in Halifax. He has written *Marriage—Restoring Our Vision* and *Collaborative Ministry* for BRF.

Stephen Rand in recent years has shared his time between Jubilee Debt Campaign, persecuted church charity Open Doors and Mainstream, a Baptist church leaders' network. He is now a grandfather to Isaac—a truly patriarchal relationship!

Veronica Zundel is an Oxford graduate, writer and journalist. She lives with her husband and son in North London, where they belong to the Mennonite Church.

Adrian Plass is a popular writer and speaker in many countries. His most recent books for BRF are *When You Walk* (revised and expanded) and *Blind Spots in the Bible*.

Stephen Cottrell is the Bishop of Reading. He has worked in parishes in London and Chichester, as Pastor of Peterborough Cathedral, as Missioner in the Wakefield diocese and as part of Springboard, the Archbishop's evangelism team.

Further BRF reading for this issue

For more in-depth coverage of some of the passages in these
Bible reading notes, we recommend the following titles:

978 1 84101 046 5, £8.99

978 1 84101 066 3, £8.99

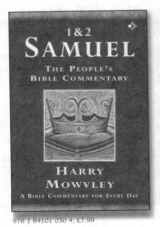

978 1 84101 030 4, £7.99

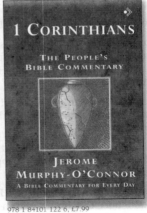

978 1 84101 122 6, £7.99

Naomi Starkey writes...

Around this time of the year I begin to make plans for future issues of *New Daylight*, looking ahead two years, so that contributors have plenty of notice as to what they will write about. It is always interesting to review past issues as I do this, and I have two very helpful spreadsheets that show contributions by books of the Bible and also by author, dating back to the first issue of *'New' Daylight* more than 20 years ago.

While the Gospels, for example, appear in every issue, some parts of the Bible, particularly in the Old Testament, are notable by their low profile. As I have probably mentioned before, I always enjoy the challenge of finding ways of drawing devotional readings from even the most obscure passages, so that *New Daylight* readers can 'boldly go' where they may not have ventured before.

Take Leviticus—the book of the Bible notorious for tripping up those who try to read all the way through from cover to cover. They make a good beginning with Genesis and Exodus, with the familiar narratives in those books. But then they come to Leviticus, and before long they grind to a halt as they try to plough through apparently impenetrable verses that seem to be the ancient equivalent of local byelaws or health and safety regulations. With this in mind (and seeing that Leviticus had not appeared in the notes since 1998),

I asked Adrian Plass to give us 'A taste of Leviticus' in this issue. I hope you will agree with me that his reflections draw out a huge amount to ponder and Leviticus will never seem so daunting again.

I'd like to welcome Amy Boucher Pye, who writes here for the first time. Her nine readings continue our journey through Mark's Gospel, which began with Rachel Boulding's readings in March, leapt forward to the events of Easter (Mark 11 and onwards) with Stephen Rand, and concludes with Stephen Cottrell on Mark 6—10 in August.

I also welcome Lisa Cherrett, who has joined me in writing on the Ten Commandments. Lisa is BRF's Project Editor, liaising with colleagues over the sub-edit (detailed grammar and spelling check), design and proofreading stages of all BRF and Barnabas publications. She also oversees our Bible reading notes publishing programme—and somehow managed to find time to contribute to *New Daylight* too!

The BRF Prayer

Almighty God,
you have taught us that your word is a lamp for our feet
and a light for our path. Help us, and all who prayerfully
read your word, to deepen our fellowship with each other
through your love. And in so doing may we come to know you
more fully, love you more truly, and follow more faithfully in
the steps of your son Jesus Christ, who lives and reigns with
you and the Holy Spirit, one God for evermore. Amen.

Jesus on the road: Mark 3—5

The three chapters in the Gospel of Mark that we will be reading this week introduce us to the fast-moving ministry of Jesus. As he brings healing and restoration to those in dire straits, news of his miracles spreads quickly. People start flocking to him, coming from all over the region to witness for themselves this unusual man and his miracles.

Jesus shows compassion as he heals, but he wants to teach the people as well, knowing that many of them are very intrigued by his more amazing acts. He shares parables—stories from everyday life—that invite his listeners to dig deeply in order to uncover the meaning. 'Listen!' he says before the parable of the sower and, afterwards, 'If anyone has ears to hear, let them hear.' Whether or not his teaching bears fruit depends on the listener.

After Jesus' teaching by the side of the lake, Mark moves on to describe several of Jesus' healings. Jesus enters Gentile territory and heals a man who has been tormented by demons for years. He then returns to a Jewish area where he restores the life of a little girl and heals a woman who has been bleeding for years. Those who have been outcasts are welcomed back into the community and given a whole new life.

Jesus' teaching and healing bring about a variety of reactions. The desperate person in peril or pain is relieved and made free. The demons acknowledge his true identity and flee. The disciples are amazed and, at times, terrified. They are forced to ask exactly who this man is that they are following. The crowds want to know more. The Pharisees and other teachers of the law are mostly incensed and so plot to kill Jesus. There is no neutral response to the Son of God.

Jesus' parables and healings all point to the kingdom of God that he is heralding. Through his life, ministry, death and rising again, Jesus is ushering in this kingdom. It is one of *shalom*, healing, restoration and new life, and it is available to all who hunger and thirst for righteousness.

In closing, I wish to acknowledge the help I received from the fine *NIV Application Commentary* by David E. Garland (Zondervan, 1996), which informed many of my comments.

Amy Boucher Pye

MARK 3:1–5 (TNIV, ABRIDGED)

Withered hearts

Jesus went into the synagogue, and a man with a shrivelled hand was there. Some of them were looking for a reason to accuse Jesus, so they watched him closely to see if he would heal him on the Sabbath… Jesus asked them, 'Which is lawful on the Sabbath: to do good or to do evil, to save life or to kill?' But they remained silent. He looked around at them in anger and, deeply distressed at their stubborn hearts, said to the man, 'Stretch out your hand.' He stretched it out, and his hand was completely restored.

Today's story follows another sabbath controversy, when the disciples were picking grain (2:23–28). Here Jesus enters the synagogue and sees not only the man with the withered hand but also those with shrivelled hearts who are wanting to accuse him.

Jesus heals the man with a simple command, unlike the healers of his time who used complicated incantations. Maimed and deformed people were barred from the temple, so his healing also ushered in social acceptance.

The Pharisees were watching Jesus' every move, for breaking the sabbath could result in death according to Old Testament law. Jesus is angry with their 'stubbornness'. The word used means a closed mind when it comes to spiritual truths. An equivalent Hebrew word is used of Pharaoh in the events of the Exodus.

Sensing their criticism, Jesus shows how he is the fulfilment of the Law. By simply speaking (and therefore not breaking the rules), he heals the man and ushers in the kingdom of God that he will be heralding in the days to come.

It's easy to caricature the Pharisees, but we too can fall into this hardness of heart. When we give up hope or insist on having our own way, we are not obeying the heavenly vision. Perhaps we've been in a relationship where we've been hurt and we fear to extend forgiveness, or something longed for hasn't materialized or we are given over to grumbling. Jesus invites us to a place of healing and restoration. Just as he said to the man, 'Stretch out your hand,' he says these words to us: 'Stretch out your heart and let me make you whole.'

Prayer

Offer a difficult situation you are facing to Jesus, asking for his healing and peace.

ABP

MARK 3:32–35 (TNIV)

Who are my family?

A crowd was sitting round [Jesus], and they told him, 'Your mother and brothers are outside looking for you.' 'Who are my mother and my brothers?' he asked. Then he looked at those seated in a circle round him and said, 'Here are my mother and my brothers! Whoever does God's will is my brother and sister and mother.'

Following yesterday's confrontation, Jesus retreats from the Pharisees and Herodians who are plotting to kill him. Even so, the crowds have heard of his amazing works and gather from far-flung places. His family, too, have heard and come 'to take charge of him', saying that 'he is out of his mind' (v. 21). The word for taking charge means to seize forcibly or arrest. We don't know why they reacted so strongly—perhaps they were worried about his safety or trying to protect their name and honour.

When Jesus hears that his mother and brothers have come for him, he responds in a way that many still find shocking. Instead of making room for them, he rejects the social structures and says that those around him, those doing the will of God, are his family. The kingdom he is ushering in is based not on blood ties, but on a shared commitment to serving God.

As a mother of small children, I have to admit that my natural allegiance is to my nuclear family. The almost fierce parenting instincts are so strong that they could turn our family into an isolated community of its own. Here, though, Jesus calls those of us living in families to come outside that shell. Our spiritual ties are to be even stronger and more lasting than those to our biological families.

In the kingdom of God, all who believe and follow are full and equal members—sisters and brothers, daughters and sons. Our commitment must be to each other —widows, single people, married couples, the elderly and the children, those who are mentally unstable. No wonder the members of the early Church shared everything and were one in heart and mind (see Acts 4:32)—they were living out this new kingdom.

We may be shocked by Jesus' words, but perhaps they can startle us out of complacency as we embrace God's definition of family.

Prayer

Lord, help me to love your sons and daughters with abandon.

ABP

Time for a soil test

'Listen! A farmer went out to sow his seed. As he was scattering the seed, some fell along the path, and the birds came and ate it up. Some fell on rocky places, where it did not have much soil. It sprang up quickly... But when the sun came up, the plants were scorched, and they withered because they had no root. Other seed fell among thorns, which grew up and choked the plants... Still other seed fell on good soil. It came up, grew and produced a crop, some multiplying thirty, some sixty, some a hundred times.'

The crowds are pursuing Jesus, so he uses a boat as a platform from which to speak (v. 1). He starts by telling parables—stories from everyday life that entail spiritual or moral lessons. Only those who seek the meaning will understand; those who are not interested will miss out.

This parable of the sower is important for it is the first of Jesus' teaching that Mark shares. Also, it's one of the few parables with an interpretation provided. It can be seen as a parable about the nature of Jesus' teaching, for if the disciples can't understand this parable, how will they understand any of them? (v. 13).

A key part is Jesus' admonition to 'listen'. This verb is similar to the one used in Deuteronomy (6:4)—'Hear, O Israel'—which was prayed daily by the Jewish people. Here, Jesus is inviting us to wake up, ponder and delve deeply. The crowds that have sprung up will quickly wither away and even the disciples in times of hardship will not stay the course. How about us?

Let us also consider the soil, for everything depends on it—not on the seed or the sower. Are we productive or unproductive soil? Jesus mentions three types that do not produce a crop and one that does.

Although soil can't change its quality, we can, thanks to the help God gives us. 'I make all things new', says the Lord (Revelation 21:5, KJV). Surely his word and the Holy Spirit dwelling in us will act as fertilizers, replacing the impurities and giving us a richness and depth that are beyond anything we could ask for or imagine.

Prayer

Lord God, make me into rich and fertile soil that yields good fruit— fruit that lasts.

ABP

A harvest of meaning

'Some people are like seed along the path, where the word is sown. As soon as they hear it, Satan comes and takes away the word... Others, like the seed sown on rocky places, hear the word and at once receive it with joy. But... when trouble or persecution comes because of the word, they quickly fall away. Still others, like seed sown among thorns, hear the word; but the worries of this life, the deceitfulness of wealth and the desires for other things come in and choke the word, making it unfruitful. Others, like seed sown on good soil, hear the word, accept it, and produce a crop—some thirty, some sixty, some a hundred times what was sown.'

When Jesus was alone with the twelve disciples, he explained the parable. Some people who hear the word of God lose it to Satan straight away. Some receive it joyfully but fall away because of persecution. Others hear the word but it is choked by wealth or worries. Still others hear and accept the word and produce a good crop.

Like any good parable, this one yields a harvest of meaning. One point, that Jesus is a lavish sower, is rooted in the Old Testament metaphor of God's work as sowing seeds (see Jeremiah 31:27–28; Hosea 2:21–23). Jesus is not concerned about 'wasting' seeds or holding any back. Instead he throws them on all types of ground in the hope that plants will spring forth. We, too, should take this lavish approach.

Another lesson is that Jesus' coming has not put an end to evil or hardship (yet). The farmer may sow many seeds, but there are forces at work in the world and in our hearts that militate against healthy plants growing from them. Sometimes the rains of disappointment come or the shiny lure of material pursuits draws us away. Trouble and persecution are still with us—but so is the Lord.

Another lesson is that God's word will produce a harvest; it will not fail. Although we may feel discouraged at the hardships we experience—individually or as a church—we should not lose hope. God is faithful and will not give up. Neither should we.

Reflection

'Sow for yourselves righteousness, reap the fruit of unfailing love, and break up your unplowed ground; for it is time to seek the Lord'
(Hosea 10:12).

ABP

The unseen farmer

'This is what the kingdom of God is like. A man scatters seed on the ground. Night and day, whether he sleeps or gets up, the seed sprouts and grows, though he does not know how. All by itself the soil produces corn—first the stalk, then the head, then the full grain in the ear. As soon as the corn is ripe, he puts the sickle to it, because the harvest has come.'

While Jesus is with the disciples, he shares more parables about the kingdom of heaven, including this one about the seed falling to the ground (only recorded in Mark). Here Jesus is pointing to what is happening under the ground with the seed, how it produces grain 'all by itself' and the farmer 'does not know how'. The word for 'by itself' is the one from which we get the English word 'automatically' and could also be translated 'without visible cause' or 'incomprehensibly'. The farmer can get on with his daily business for the seed has the power within itself to grow.

Through this parable, Jesus is telling the disciples that the kingdom of God is hidden and humble. Although we may not observe any new signs of life, we can still be confident that God is at work under the surface. There are unseen powers under God's control that are real and effective.

Growth, too, comes in stages—first the stalk, then the head, then the full grain. We cannot rush the plant along or skip any phases of growth for each is necessary and happens in its own time. I see this principle working itself out daily as my one-year-old daughter is taking her first steps. It is true for our spiritual walk, too.

Are you discouraged about how you are living your life? Do you want to make changes but don't seem able to do so? Perhaps you're concerned for a loved one—a parent, child, friend, spouse—who is suffering or living apart from God's purposes. Know from this parable that God is at work bringing about his harvest. Even though we do not know how the seed will grow, he will spark it into life. His purposes will not fail.

Prayer

Lord Jesus, when I'm discouraged, help me to see you bringing about your glory.

ABP

MARK 4:37–41 (TNIV)

Even the wind obeys

A furious squall came up, and the waves broke over the boat, so that it was nearly swamped. Jesus was in the stern, sleeping on a cushion. The disciples woke him and said to him, 'Teacher, don't you care if we drown?' He got up, rebuked the wind and said to the waves, 'Quiet! Be still!' Then the wind died down and it was completely calm. He said to his disciples, 'Why are you so afraid? Do you still have no faith?' They were terrified and asked each other, 'Who is this? Even the wind and the waves obey him!'

In our fast-paced look at Jesus' ministry, we move from parables to miracles. The first occurs at the end of a long day of teaching, when he and his disciples cross the Sea of Galilee. Although many were fishermen, they still were terrified when a storm developed and nearly capsized the boat. Jesus slept peacefully while all this was going on and, in desperation, they woke him up. Not yet fully realizing who he was, they were stunned when with a single word he stilled the storm.

The word that Jesus uses to bring order is the one that he employs when he tells demons to be quiet (see Mark 1:23–27). It's a firm and forceful phrase—literally 'Be muzzled!' As with the demons, the sea obeys its master immediately.

You would think the disciples would be cheered by the newfound calm, but, instead, they are startled. They are starting to come to a deeper understanding of who Jesus is, perhaps making connections between him and Old Testament passages on God as creator and calmer of the seas (such as Psalm 89:9: 'You rule over the surging sea; when its waves mount up, you still them').

It's during the storms that our own faith can be most tested: a diagnosis of cancer, betrayal by a friend, losing a job… We may know intellectually the many assurances of God's love and care, but, when the winds are roaring, we easily forget. Our almost reflexive cry is to Jesus, and he is there. Although he doesn't promise that we will be storm-free, he does promise that he will never leave nor forsake us.

Reflection

'When you pass through the waters, I will be with you; and when you pass through the rivers, they will not sweep over you' (Isaiah 43:2).

ABP

MARK 5:2–13 (TNIV, ABRIDGED)

Out of his mind

A man with an evil spirit came from the tombs to meet [Jesus]. This man lived in the tombs… Night and day among the tombs and in the hills he would cry out and cut himself with stones. When he saw Jesus… he ran and fell on his knees in front of him. He shouted at the top of his voice, "What do you want with me, Jesus, Son of the Most High God? In God's name don't torture me!' For Jesus had said to him, 'Come out of this man, you evil spirit!' … A large herd of pigs was feeding on the nearby hillside. The demons begged Jesus, 'Send us among the pigs…' He gave them permission, and the evil spirits came out and went into the pigs.

Today begins a trilogy of miracles that Jesus performed for desperate people. The first is the expulsion of demons from a man who had been consigned to the tombs, an utter outcast. Although the townspeople had tried to tie him down (vv. 3–4), the demonic forces within would break any chain.

Unlike other encounters between Jesus and demons, here Jesus has an extended exchange and, as a result, the demons see his divine nature and use his true name. Perhaps not wanting to leave familiar territory, they ask to be sent among a herd of pigs. Jesus consents and the pigs fling themselves down the hillside and are drowned (v. 13).

Earlier, Jesus was telling parables of the coming kingdom; now he is acting them out as he brings restoration and wholeness. Later (vv. 15–20), the delivered man wants to become Jesus' disciple, but Jesus tells him to go home and share what he has done for him (probably because he was a Gentile—a hint of the spreading of the kingdom to come). The townspeople, in contrast, want Jesus to leave.

Jesus shows his authority over not only the wind and waves but also legions of demons. Imagine yourself as part of the story. How would you react as one of the townspeople? A disciple? The possessed man? How do you, two millennia later, respond?

For reflection

'Guard my life, for I am faithful to you; save your servant who trusts in you. You are my God; have mercy on me, Lord, for I call to you all day long' (Psalm 86:2–3).

ABP

A healing sandwich

One of the synagogue leaders, named Jairus, came, and when he saw Jesus, he fell at his feet. He pleaded earnestly with him, 'My little daughter is dying. Please come and put your hands on her so that she will be healed and live.' So Jesus went with him... Some people came from the house of Jairus... 'Your daughter is dead,' they said. 'Why bother the teacher any more?' Overhearing what they said, Jesus told him, 'Don't be afraid; just believe.'

Today's reading provides the bread for a 'Markan sandwich', in which the filling is tomorrow's story. Here Mark starts the account of Jairus seeking healing for his daughter, then tells of the woman who touches Jesus to find healing (vv. 25–34) and, finally, returns to Jairus and his daughter. This is not the first time he creates such a sandwich and many commentators think that he does it to link the meanings of the two stories.

Jairus is one of the few people actually named in the Gospels besides the disciples. As a synagogue leader, he is a man of social standing, but he is desperate for help. His 12-year-old girl is near death and he wants Jesus to 'come and put [his] hands on her' so that she will live. Like the woman who touches Jesus' cloak, he believes that healing will come through his touch.

Jairus' faith is tested as Jesus agrees to come but is delayed by the haemorrhaging woman. Then, people from his household inform him of his daughter's death. They carry on to his home and, when they get there, funeral proceedings are under way (v. 38). But Jesus tells him not to be afraid and to believe—and he does. He is then astonished when Jesus heals his daughter (vv. 41–43).

As we see, faith can come in various shapes and sizes. It can be as tiny as a mustard seed and still achieve amazing things. Somehow, in the economy of God, he takes our pitiful belief and multiplies it mightily, to his glory. We simply need to look to him—Father, Son and Holy Spirit—and he will enlarge our faith, helping us to act on it and hang on to it even when we meet obstacles that threaten to overwhelm us.

Reflection
'Lord, I believe; help my unbelief!'
(Mark 9:24, NKJV)

ABP

Making all things new

A woman was there who had been subject to bleeding for twelve years. She had suffered a great deal under the care of many doctors and had spent all she had, yet instead of getting better she grew worse. When she heard about Jesus, she came up behind him in the crowd and touched his cloak, because she thought, 'If I just touch his clothes, I will be healed.' Immediately her bleeding stopped and she felt in her body that she was freed from her suffering.

The third in this trilogy of miracles is a woman who has bled for twelve years, probably from uterine haemorrhaging. This bleeding makes her unclean according to Old Testament Law and, thus, she is considered an outcast and hopes for marriage and a family have been quashed. She has unsuccessfully sought medical help, spending all her money on trying to find a cure.

Finally, she hears about Jesus and his miracles and, just making contact with his clothes with her fingers, she is healed. She hasn't reckoned on Jesus sensing that power has gone out from him, though, so she is surprised when he demands to know who has touched him. Fearing the worst, she comes forward and is amazed to hear not an admonishment but that her faith has healed her (vv. 33–34).

As noted yesterday, this story is the 'filling' in the healing sandwich, which implies that there are links between this story and that of Jairus' daughter. A central one is the faith of Jairus and this woman, which endured trials but was used by Jesus to bring about healing.

Another connection is that Jesus is concerned with all in society. The two people he healed were female. He did not save his *shalom* for the more 'respected' people, namely men. Also, Jesus was not defiled by the ceremonial uncleanness of those he healed, even though he touched them. He does not shrink away from the lowly and oppressed.

Healing, faith, restoration, *shalom*—these are the new foundation stones of the kingdom Jesus is building. We, too, can share in this kingdom as we bring our impure thoughts and motives, callous hearts and heartless actions before the healer and redeemer who loves us, forgives us and makes us whole.

Prayer

Jesus, in you I live and move and have my being. Make me whole, that I may share your love with others.

ABP

The Ten Commandments (Exodus 20)

Mention Exodus chapter 20 to any average member of the public and they will almost certainly look blank. Mention the Ten Commandments and, these days, some will probably still look blank, but more people will be able to come up with a few 'Thou shalt nots'. While more than a few churches have the Ten Commandments displayed prominently somewhere, perhaps—in an Anglican church—on the wall behind the Communion table, they are no longer likely to be found in the average primary school.

Like the Seven Deadly Sins, the Ten Commandments (or 'Decalogue', to use their formal name from the Greek—literally 'ten words') have had a cultural impact beyond the confines of the Church. They encapsulate principles that still underpin what we understand by the phrase 'civilized society'. Read the comment in any Sunday newspaper and you will find something about the importance of taking a break, caring for older people, reducing crime, building up communal trust. Evangelist J. John has developed a successful series of outreach events, *Just 10*, based on the relevance of the Ten Commandments to people's lives today.

At the same time, these 'ten words' are from a far-off time and place, remote from our own experience. As always, especially when reading the Old Testament, it is important to have some understanding of the original context. This can help us not only to avoid misunderstandings but also to enhance our grasp of the nuances of the Commandments themselves. Scholars have pointed out similarities between them and treaties from this era and that Moses, educated at the Egyptian court, may well have been aware of such treaties. This covenant, though, is made with God himself. It may well be no coincidence that it shares characteristics with, for example, Hittite covenants. After all, God was revealing himself to a particular people at a particular time, so he would surely use the kind of approach with which they were likely to be familiar. Here's a thought: how would he reveal the commandments to us today?

To help us get to grips with the Ten Commandments, we will explore links between them and some of what Jesus said about various aspects of the Law, remembering always how he declared that he had come 'not to abolish... but to fulfil' (see Matthew 5:17).

Naomi Starkey and Lisa Cherrett

No other gods

And God spoke all these words: 'I am the Lord your God, who brought you out of Egypt, out of the land of slavery. You shall have no other gods before me.'

Right at the very start, before God declares the first commandment of all, we are given the context for the whole of this covenant. It is far more than some interesting background point to note—here, the context explains the heart of the covenant.

The God who is making this treaty is not just another local deity, a territorial spirit of the forbiddingly desolate wilderness where the Israelites are camped. Nor does he belong to the Egyptian pantheon—Ra, the sun god, Thoth (god of wisdom) or, perhaps, Osiris (god of the dead). Nor is he one of the Canaanite fertility gods, Baal or Dagon. This God is the LORD (the capital letters standing for the untranslatable Hebrew YHWH, which we will consider further on Tuesday). More than that, he is the God who has saved them from slavery and the threat of genocide just three months earlier. Like a divine midwife, he has delivered them into a new life and now they are to learn how that life should be led.

This God, the one LORD God, is the one who rescues. He did not demand covenant obedience as a condition of rescuing the people, but only once they had been freed. He offered them the chance to respond in gratitude to what he had done for them, which itself was in response to an earlier covenant: 'The Israelites groaned in their slavery... God heard their groaning and he remembered his covenant with Abraham, with Isaac and with Jacob. So God looked on the Israelites and was concerned about them' (Exodus 2:23–25). What he did want, however, was their undivided love.

When we turn to the New Testament, we see the same saving impulse at work. As Jesus told Nicodemus: 'For God so loved the world that he gave his one and only Son, that whoever believes in him shall not perish but have eternal life' (John 3:16). Our God—Father, Son, Spirit—is a saviour. As Jesus remarked a few chapters later, 'I and the Father are one' (10:30).

Reflection

If God had not delivered the Israelites from slavery, what might have happened?

NS

Making images

'You shall not make for yourself an image in the form of anything in heaven above or on the earth beneath or in the waters below. You shall not bow down to them or worship them; for I, the Lord your God, am a jealous God, punishing the children for the sin of the parents to the third and fourth generation of those who hate me, but showing love to a thousand generations of those who love me and keep my commandments.'

Over the centuries, the banning of images in worship led to Christians destroying icons and paintings and smashing statues and stained-glass windows. They feared that worship of the creator would be replaced by worship of created objects. What was lost in the process was the chance to worship through the senses rather than the intellect alone, something that parts of the Church are still rediscovering.

In the ancient Near East, honouring the household gods with elaborate rituals was an integral part of life, caricatured in Isaiah 44: 'Half of the wood [the carpenter] burns in the fire; over it he prepares his meal… From the rest he makes a god, his idol' (vv. 16–17). 'The LORD your God' demanded that his people lift their eyes beyond the visible world to acknowledge his authority.

We may find it difficult to think of God as 'jealous', thinking that he should be above such an emotion, but, if the human race is truly made in God's image, why should he not be emotional? As we read the scriptures, we hear God speaking not in the measured tones of a High Court judge, but as an anguished husband, despairing that his wife, whom he chose and cherished, has betrayed him repeatedly.

We may struggle even more with the idea of God punishing the descendants of those who reject him. If we reread the words, however, we start to see a different picture: God's mercy is such that he plans to limit the damaging consequences of rejecting him, while continuing to shower love on the 'thousand generations' of those who observe the covenant faithfully.

Reflection

'No one can serve two masters. Either you will hate the one and love the other, or you will be devoted to the one and despise the other. You cannot serve both God and Money' (Luke 16:13).

NS

Blasphemy

'You shall not misuse the name of the Lord your God, for the Lord will not hold anyone guiltless who misuses his name.'

In *People's Bible Commentary: Exodus* (BRF, 2006), Hugh Page reminds us how names are a particularly powerful type of word. In Genesis 1:1—2:3, God names—and thereby brings into being—the whole of creation. At the start of John's Gospel, we find Jesus named as the Word of God, the supreme creative force: 'In the beginning was the Word... Through him all things were made' (1:1, 3).

In Exodus 6:2–3, God spells out to Moses how the holy name defines who he is: 'I am the LORD [*YHWH*]. I appeared to Abraham, to Isaac and to Jacob as God Almighty [in Hebrew, *El-Shaddai*], but by my name the LORD I did not make myself known'. While the Hebrew for 'I am' sounds similar to YHWH (as in 3:13–14, where God describes himself as 'I am'), it is not certain that this is the name's meaning. Jesus made use of this similarity at times (see, for example, John 8:58), underlining his true origin and often provoking outrage from his hearers.

Here is a Hebrew lesson. YHWH are the Hebrew consonants that represent God's name (also known as the Tetragrammaton, from the Greek for 'word with four letters'). As God's name was considered too sacred to utter, readers said 'Adonai' (the Lord) when they encountered YHWH in a text. The vowels from 'Adonai' were added to YHWH as a reminder and later Christians wrongly read the word as 'Yahweh' or 'Jehovah'. God's name is not Jehovah; it is a mystery, but a mystery that we can enter into, if not fully understand, if we trust him as Saviour, YHWH, who delivers his people.

The command, then, is to treat his holy name with due reverence. We have no room here to begin a discussion about blasphemy laws. Instead, we can ask ourselves if we are ever prone to overfamiliarity, so immersed in our personal issues that we forget who God truly is. Do we misuse the LORD's name by using it as a kind of 'divine seal of approval' for our own agendas without first humbly seeking his will?

Prayer

Holy God, may we never forget to pause at times and ponder your majesty.

NS

Keeping the sabbath

'Remember the Sabbath day by keeping it holy. Six days you shall labour and do all your work, but the seventh day is a sabbath to the Lord your God. On it you shall not do any work, neither you, nor your son or daughter, nor your male or female servant, nor your animals, nor any foreigner residing in your towns. For in six days the Lord made the heavens and the earth, the sea, and all that is in them, but he rested on the seventh day. Therefore the Lord blessed the Sabbath day and made it holy.'

In Laura Ingalls Wilder's *Little House in the Big Woods* (1932), we find a vivid evocation of old-fashioned sabbath-keeping: no work, but also no playing, laughing, smiling, talking, cooking or hitching up horses (so you had to walk to church). Children were expected to sit motionless through a two-hour sermon, followed by an afternoon studying their catechism. The day of rest was the most dreary day of the week—a travesty of what this commandment was intended to achieve.

These verses were addressed to people who had recently escaped slavery, after years of being cruelly worked by whip-wielding overseers, with no chance of developing any sense of a good work/life balance. Accordingly, God showed them how they, and all within their household (even the animals), should enshrine the principle of a day of rest.

That this principle became distorted into endless petty rules and regulations is clear from Jesus' comments on keeping the sabbath, which, predictably, scandalized the religious authorities. He emphasized the fact that 'the Sabbath was made for people, not people for the Sabbath' (Mark 2:27); the commandment was intended to liberate, not stifle, the human heart.

While legislation in favour of 24/7 shopping has done much (in the UK) to destroy the peace of our traditional day of rest, we can still resist the pressure to be doing/buying/achieving every minute of every week. This commandment asks that we create regular spaces for rest from busyness of all kinds, where we can be free to seek God's presence and nurture our tired spirit.

Reflection

'[We must] mount a constant guard at the gates of our heart against our relentless refusal to rest.'

David Shepherd, *Seeking Sabbath* (BRF, 2007)

NS

Honouring parents

'Honour your father and your mother, so that you may live long in the land the Lord your God is giving you.'

As many a preacher has been fond of pointing out, this is the only one of the Ten Commandments explicitly linked to a promise. If the people care for their parents, they can hope to enjoy a long life in the promised land. We find a similar promise in Deuteronomy, linked to obedience to the covenant as a whole: 'I set before you today life and prosperity, death and destruction... Now choose life, so that you and your children may live... and [the LORD] will give you many years in the land he swore to give to your fathers' (see 30:15–20).

Again, we should remember that the Israelites had just escaped from desperate, brutalizing circumstances. When a nation undergoes severe trauma, it can take generations for the resulting emotional wounds to heal (witness the struggles of the Inuit in the Arctic, Australian Aborigines and Native Americans). Maybe that is why the LORD spells out the link between treatment of the elders (likely to have been considered of little worth in a slave-based economy) and the hope of future security and prosperity, for, if children see parents modelling such care, they are more likely to do likewise in the course of time.

In ancient Israel, as in many cultures today, family life was central. It was the place where you belonged and where your unquestioning loyalty was due. By contrast, we are more likely to think of family as the cocoon from which we emerge into adult life. Sadly, for all too many, it can be a profoundly damaging environment. How can the commandment apply in such situations?

Jesus provided a startlingly different perspective on family. When his own mother and brothers turned up one day for a quiet word, pointing to his disciples, he said, 'Whoever does God's will is my brother and sister and mother' (Mark 3:35). Membership of the kingdom of the new covenant brings with it membership of the family of God, of which earthly families are no more than the palest of copies, and where all can belong, sheltered by the loving care of our Father in heaven.

Prayer
Loving Father, show us what it means to honour our parents.

NS

Murder

You shall not murder... 'You have heard that it was said to the people long ago, "You shall not murder, and anyone who murders will be subject to judgment." But I tell you that anyone who is angry with a brother or sister will be subject to judgment. Again, anyone who says to a brother or sister, "Raca", is answerable to the Sanhedrin. And anyone who says, "You fool!" will be in danger of the fire of hell.'

The prohibition of murder needs no explanation. One six-year-old in Sunday school, on hearing this commandment, sucked in her breath and muttered, 'Ooh, no, no, no'—and most of us would share her instinctive horror at the very idea. In British law, murder is the deliberate unlawful killing of a fellow human being (though our lawmakers debate the meanings of 'deliberate', 'unlawful' and even 'human being'). The Hebrew word used in Exodus 20 is more comprehensive, referring to all kinds of killing, premeditated and otherwise (see Hugh Page, *PBC Exodus*).

These arguments about definitions, though, can distract us from Jesus' teaching that a sinful attitude is, in God's judgment, just as wicked as the action to which it may lead. Some forms of anger are justified—for example, against injustice and cruelty. Jesus himself expressed anger at the desecration of the temple (John 2:15). However, the kind of anger he condemns in Matthew is the kind that damages the vulnerable soul, the psychological essence of a human individual, which is as prone to injury as the body. 'Raca' is an Aramaic term of contempt (as the footnote in the NIV tells us) and contempt for another person's life, physical or psychological, is the root of murder.

It's interesting that Jesus talks of anger and insults directed at a 'brother or sister'. The first murder recorded in the Bible was the murder of a brother (Genesis 4:8) and it is often the people closest to us who can make us angriest. Yet, whether we are annoyed by a close friend or relative or a faceless service provider at the end of a phone line, we should avoid the harsh rebuke, the wounding retort or the contemptuous insult that crushes another's soul.

Prayer

If you can, read William Blake's poem 'The poison tree'. Confess any untold anger and ask forgiveness.

LC

Adultery

You shall not commit adultery… [Jesus said] 'You have heard that it was said, "You shall not commit adultery." But I tell you that anyone who looks at a woman lustfully has already committed adultery with her in his heart.'

Marriage—a relationship in which a man and a woman vow lifelong sexual fidelity to each other—is the bedrock of a stable society, and this remains as true today as it was in Old Testament times. Therefore, adultery—a sexual act between two people, one at least of whom is married to someone else—will have a shattering effect on that stability.

In the individualistic culture of today's Western world, we tend to underestimate the effects of our actions on others. In fact, all of our actions are like a stone thrown into a pond: the ripples spread out and wash over every person whose life touches our own, bringing either disturbance or refreshment. When the covenant of marriage is broken by the act of adultery, the effects can be more like the underwater earthquake that unleashes a tsunami. It explodes the trust that existed between the partners involved, wounds the children of the marriage and splinters the networks of loyalty that bind together families and friends.

So, does it seem surprising that Jesus should be so strict about a fleeting lustful glance? The trouble is, of course, that adultery begins in the eyes and the mind. True marriage is a psychological as well as a physical union. Here again we see that, in God's judgment, mind and body are intertwined and inseparable from each other.

I once had the deeply unpleasant experience of being constantly stared at by a man sitting opposite me while I was travelling on the London Underground. After many uncomfortable minutes, he looked away with an expression and sound of disgust. Of course, I can't be sure what had been passing through his mind, but I felt as if I had been used and then kicked into the gutter. Lust, like the kind of anger we thought about yesterday, is a sign of indifference to the precious individuality of the other person—a desire to possess the body without cherishing the soul.

Reflection

'We take captive every thought to make it obedient to Christ'
(2 Corinthians 10:5).

LC

Exodus 20:15; Luke 3:11–14a (TNIV)

Theft

You shall not steal... John answered, 'Anyone who has two shirts should share with the one who has none, and anyone who has food should do the same.' Even tax collectors came to be baptized. 'Teacher,' they asked, 'what should we do?' 'Don't collect any more than you are required to,' he told them. Then some soldiers asked him, 'And what should we do?' He replied, 'Don't extort money.'

The first thing we can notice about the eighth commandment is that, in God's eyes, people have a right to own property and enjoy it without fear of loss by theft. This may seem to be at odds with Acts 4:32, where we're told that, among the first Christians, 'No one claimed that any of their possessions was their own, but they shared everything they had.' In this kind of community, there can be no theft because there is no such thing as personal property to steal.

In Luke 3, however, John the Baptist brings his trademark blunt wisdom to bear on the question. There may be two sides to the coin of this commandment: we are forbidden to take without permission what belongs to another person or to defraud others, but we are also urged to be generous with our own possessions, so that the needy do not feel under pressure to steal in order to survive.

At the heart of the command, whatever our circumstances, is the call to preserve trust throughout society: 'Do not plot harm against your neighbour, who lives trustfully near you,' says Proverbs 3:29. If we believe that God provides the necessities of life, we can start by developing a carefree trust in him for the things we need and the generosity to work with him by providing for others. The temptation to work against him by depriving others of his provision for them may then become less powerful.

Possessions do not carry financial value alone. Possessions carry meanings for us: they represent the wherewithal to complete daily tasks or rewards for work done, or reminders of loved ones, or beauty to be enjoyed. That is why burglary is emotionally violating. To share these precious things by common consent, as the early Christians did, is a great gift; to be deprived of them by theft is soul-destroying.

Prayer

Help me, Lord, to trust you and to be trustworthy in everything.

LC

False witness

You shall not give false testimony against your neighbour... '[The devil] was a murderer from the beginning, not holding to the truth, for there is no truth in him. When he lies, he speaks his native language, for he is a liar and the father of lies.'

The context of Exodus 20:16 is a formal court setting, in which someone is being tried for a criminal offence. In Israelite society, steps were taken to guard against false testimony. A person could not be convicted of a crime on the word of a single witness—two or three were required (Deuteronomy 19:15).

The prophet Zechariah adds a further dimension to this commandment: 'Speak the truth... render in your gates judgments that are true and make for peace' (8:16, NRSV). Peace is certainly in short supply when one tells lies about another: the sense of outrage is immense and can lead to long-term strife.

In every arena where we come into conflict, not just the law courts, we may face the temptation to give false testimony, whether it be to get our frightened selves out of trouble, misguidedly shelter a guilty third party or even snatch the chance of bringing about an enemy's downfall. Whatever our motivation for the sin, here is yet another commandment that aims to preserve cohesion between neighbours. Trust, peace and justice are all undermined by false witness and the outcome for the falsely accused can be devastating, whether it's the loss of life (where capital punishment is legal) or the loss of reputation (as the gossips whisper, 'There's no smoke without fire').

As John 8 tells us, however, the conflict between truth and lies goes even deeper than the foundations of human communities. God and Satan stand opposed to each other on these grounds more clearly than any other except the opposition between life and death. God is the giver of life; Satan is 'a murderer'. God speaks the truth (Isaiah 45:19); Satan is 'the father of lies'. If we wish to be on God's side in the cosmic struggle that is so often played out on earth, truth must be the belt that holds all our heavenly armour in place against the devil's attacks (Ephesians 6:14).

Prayer

God of truth and peace, please give me the courage to oppose lies and discord, even if it is at personal cost.

LC

EXODUS 20:17; LUKE 12:15 (TNIV)

You shall not covet

You shall not covet your neighbour's house. You shall not covet your neighbour's wife, or his male or female servant, his ox or donkey, or anything that belongs to your neighbour... [Jesus] said to them, 'Watch out! Be on your guard against all kinds of greed; life does not consist in an abundance of possessions.'

When I was a child, our parents bought a swing and set it up in our garden. The little girl next door, watching the proceedings, asked how high the swing was and we informed her that it was 9 feet tall. She gazed up at her own swing for a moment, then turned and said, 'I think *ours* is 9 foot 2!'

What is it in human nature that urges us to stay those two inches ahead of our neighbour? Certainly, advertisers feed on our drive to compare and compete, bombarding us with covetable images. Everything in our culture is 'graded': our postcode, the make and model of our car, the quality of our clothes, even the supermarket where we buy our food, all position us on a social scale. So we learn to value people in material terms, too, replacing gratitude, contentment and generosity with the stresses brought by greed.

The things that we're forbidden to covet in Exodus may sound rather quaint—the wife, servants and farm animals. As signs of prosperity and self-sufficiency, though, they are the Old Testament equivalent of the house, car, food and clothes with which we display our success. (Think of Jacob surrounded by his family, servants and herds: Genesis 30:26, 43.)

Material things promise fulfilment, but they fail to deliver. I mentioned previously that possessions carry emotional meanings as well as financial value, so there is a great danger that we invest more in them than is good for us. Psalm 62:10 says, 'Though your riches increase, do not set your heart on them.' Jesus gave many warnings about the desire to get rich, including Luke 12:15 in our passage above, and he echoes the psalmist: 'For where your treasure is, there your heart will be also' (Matthew 6:21).

Again, this commandment is about guarding our inner life—our 'heart', the essence of our being—and removing the stress of being in unceasing competition with others.

Reflection

Why not spend a day practising contentment and generosity?

LC

Love

One of the teachers of the law... asked him, 'Of all the commandments, which is the most important?' 'The most important one,' answered Jesus, 'is this: "Hear, O Israel: the Lord our God, the Lord is one. Love the Lord your God with all your heart and with all your soul and with all your mind and with all your strength." The second is this: "Love your neighbour as yourself."'

When asked to name the most important commandment, Jesus does not choose one of the ten. Instead, he uses Deuteronomy 6:4–5 and Leviticus 19:18 to sum up the spirit of the Law. Mark's account includes the *Shema*, the most important Jewish prayer: 'Hear, O Israel... the Lord is one.' The word 'one' here could mean 'unique' (the only God) or 'whole, undivided'. The latter definition gives us a clue to the nature of God's love: nothing about God can be half-baked, insincere or diluted.

As Naomi explained in the introduction, God's commands are part of his covenant with his people, in which he takes the lead and we respond: 'We love because he first loved us' (1 John 4:19). The kind of love he looks for in response from us is like his own: passionate, whole-hearted, unwavering in its devotion. If we love God and love other people like this, we will keep the Ten Commandments without even trying. We will honour and worship God above every other spiritual rival and we will do nothing to harm our neighbours.

The result of such love, worked out through the whole of society, would be freedom from fear or suspicion, physical safety, tranquillity, contentment and harmonious relations between neighbours and nations—all qualities that are included in *shalom*. This Hebrew word is usually translated as 'peace', but its root meaning has to do with wholeness or completeness.

All these ideas are, of course, related to each other. The Lord our God is one—complete and undivided. He asks us to respond to him with a similarly undivided love that consumes our entire being, and such love extended to our neighbour will result in a completeness of well-being and peace in society.

Prayer

Come down, O love divine, seek thou this soul of mine, and visit it with thine own ardour glowing.

Bianco da Siena (d. 1434)

LC

The Holy Spirit

Reading about God's Holy Spirit is a bit like listening to our own heartbeat. The Spirit is not outside us and far away, but within us, shaping our lives and the worship we give. Even as our eyes scan the page, the Spirit waits at our shoulder, prompting our mind and stirring our heart to faith and prayer. Reading about the Holy Spirit is also like looking over a photograph album with a close relative or friend. We see our relationship more clearly, as we notice it developing through the years. We are grateful for all we have received, and we glimpse more of what our friendship might become.

The story of God's Holy Spirit begins on the first page of the Bible, where the Spirit appears as God's creative energy, powerful and tender, lively and life-giving. Our Old Testament readings show us the Spirit's work in creation and people who were given a special role by God. Then we begin to look forward, as prophets speak of the Spirit's coming in a new way— first in a godly king, then spreading across the earth.

This takes us to the New Testament—first to Jesus, in whom the prophecy of a Spirit-anointed king finds an echo and an answer. From Jesus we follow the story to Pentecost (the first Whitsun) and on through the growing churches of the book of Acts. Finally, we read two short passages from Romans. These show us the most personal aspect of the Spirit's work, as the 'go-between', connecting and interpreting a troubled world to the very heart of God.

From God's good creation and the Spirit breathing on the waters, we travel round to God's aching world and the sighing of the Spirit in the believer's heart. Potential and pain, hope and hurt, glory and grief, are all part of the Holy Spirit's story and these are part of our own stories, too, part of the course of your life and mine. We do not meet the Spirit as a stranger, but as someone whose own story resonates with ours and who knows us from within.

The Spirit starts at creation, but we shall go there on day two. The first day of our readings is Ascension and this, in its own way, celebrates the Spirit of God. As Jesus leaves, it is time to meet the Holy Spirit.

John Proctor

ACTS 1:6–9 (NRSV)

Power point

> So when [the apostles] had come together, they asked him, 'Lord, is this the time when you will restore the kingdom to Israel?' He replied, 'It is not for you to know the times or periods that the Father has set by his own authority. But you will receive power when the Holy Spirit has come upon you; and you will be my witnesses in Jerusalem, in all Judea and Samaria, and to the ends of the earth.' When he had said this, as they were watching, he was lifted up, and a cloud took him out of their sight.

Ascension is a good moment to start thinking about God's Holy Spirit. Jesus' ascension was the moment that made it possible for us to know the Spirit. When Jesus ascended, the Spirit came to continue his work, to touch his people with power, breathe life and love into the world. When Jesus left his friends, he did not abandon them but released his presence in a new way. His people would discover a fuller confidence in their faith and fresh energy for service.

'Will you restore the kingdom?' asked the disciples. It sounds from Jesus' response as if he was saying, 'Think again' or 'Not yet', but maybe he meant, 'Yes, I will restore the kingdom—through you.' The world would experience the loving rule of God. Healing power would flow. Good news would be given and many people would be transformed by it. Hope would break into life, like a carpet of flowers in the spring sunshine. This would be the kingdom—not complete, but on its way; not for Israel only, but for the other nations, too, and this would happen through people who trusted Jesus, a fragile company of disciples, stirred into life by the breath of God.

Ascension is easy to overlook. In Britain, it's not a public holiday. Many churches do not hold a service on it and, by Sunday, the moment has past. Yet, in a sense, the moment is never past for it is the point from which power flows: 'if I do not go away, the Advocate will not come to you; but if I go, I will send him to you' (John 16:7). Ascension releases the Spirit and the Spirit has never left.

Prayer

Lord, may we be part of your coming kingdom, by the strength of your Spirit.

JP

Kiss of life

In the beginning when God created the heavens and the earth, the earth was a formless void and darkness covered the face of the deep, while a wind from God swept over the face of the waters. Then God said, 'Let there be light'; and there was light. And God saw that the light was good; and God separated the light from the darkness. God called the light Day, and the darkness he called Night. And there was evening, and there was morning, the first day.

Yesterday, we read of Jesus' ascension. In the days to come, we follow the story of God's Spirit in the long era of preparation that led up to Jesus. Today's verses come from the very dawn of creation. They take us into a dark and empty world, without light or shape or substance, yet, through the chaos and gloom, we feel the breath ruffling the waters and sense the promise of things to come. God is stirring.

'A mighty wind' says one version of the Bible. There are different ways to make sense of the ancient Hebrew words, but probably 'wind from God', 'Spirit of God' or even 'breath of God' are better translations. This is a purposeful, creative movement. The Spirit broods on the waters, as a mother bird hovers over her nest, protecting and nurturing the young life within (Deuteronomy 32:11). Out of darkness, light and hope come gradually into view. God's world will be whole, lovely and true, rich with potential and possibility.

Wherever we encounter the Spirit of God, we need not talk of a visitor, a strange and disturbing presence on earth, for the Spirit breathed this world into life. The wholesome energy of creation, the world's complexity and beauty, life's majesty and mystery are the fingerprints of the Spirit. All that the Spirit goes on doing—everything we read in scripture, all we know of the Spirit in our own lives—is part of this same glad story.

The Spirit who shaped creation is at home here, rejoicing in the world's goodness and working to restore its people to the God who made us. To walk with God's Spirit is to live within an old, old story of a fertile, fruitful, fragile world and a faithful God.

Prayer

Creator Spirit, breathe your life into us, day by day.

JP

Panorama of praise

O Lord, how manifold are your works! In wisdom you have made them all; the earth is full of your creatures. Yonder is the sea, great and wide, creeping things innumerable are there, living things both small and great… When you hide your face, they are dismayed; when you take away their breath, they die and return to their dust. When you send forth your spirit, they are created; and you renew the face of the ground.

This psalm is a grand tour of creation. Read it from start to finish and the world is spread before you—skies and seas, sunshine and shadows, sounds and seasons. Filled with reverence and rejoicing, the writer leads us around the earth and invites us to lift our hearts to God. For corn, wine and oil, thank God. For high trees, where birds build safely, praise be. For the sea, with its waves and waters, ships and shoals, blessings on the name of the Lord. For creatures that crawl and creep, for beasts that bark and bray, give honour and glory to our Maker. This is God's world, and God is worth praising for it.

Today's verses come towards the end of the psalm. God's works are many and great, says the psalmist, as he turns his face upwards in prayer. The world is marvellous and strange, heavy with mystery and rich with plenty. It is also utterly dependent. It lives because God lives and because God shares his life with it. God's work of creation is not the winding of a clock, which is then left to itself, but a continuing process, a constant act of care, a steady breathing of strength and newness into a decaying and dependent world.

Creatures die. Our spirit, the animating power that makes us alive, will eventually leave our bodies and we shall go back to dust. God's Spirit, though, does not grow tired. God's breath never runs short. The world is infused with life, day by day, year on year, generation on generation, constantly older and yet ever new. God's Spirit is alive, at work and at large. Praise be!

Reflection and prayer

All that is new, around us and within us—the light of day, the scents of summer, strength and faith and breath—is a gift of God's Spirit, who deserves our glad praise.

JP

Gifts for the giver

Then Moses said to the Israelites: See, the Lord has called by name Bezalel son of Uri son of Hur... he has filled him with divine spirit, with skill, intelligence, and knowledge... to devise artistic designs, to work in gold, silver, and bronze, in cutting stones for setting, and in carving wood, in every kind of craft. And he has inspired him to teach, both him and Oholiab son of Ahisamach, of the tribe of Dan. He has filled them with skill to do every kind of work done by an artisan or by a designer or by an embroiderer in blue, purple, and crimson yarns, and in fine linen, or by a weaver—by any sort of artisan or skilled designer.

Our last two readings spoke of God's Spirit as the breath of creation, shaping and sustaining the world's life. Now we see the gifts of creation offered back to God in praise. As the people of Israel crossed the desert on the Exodus journey, they built a tabernacle. This portable place of worship was a focal point for their faith, a reminder that God journeyed beside them.

The means to make it beautiful were gifts from God, whose Spirit inspired the creativity, craft and care of those who would direct and design the work. What these people offered, of hand and eye and thought and time, was not just a work of skill but spiritual service, too. They enabled people to connect with God. Cutting and carving, texture and tapestry, gold and gems, served and strengthened the faith of the whole community.

Christian worship also reflects many gifts and skills. Songs and speech, sound and silence, art and image, all help us to praise. The people who design and build our churches, cut wood and glass, arrange fabric and flowers, share drama or dance, translate the Bible and write the Church's prayers—all of them bring us blessings from God and open us to God. The Spirit breathed life into the world and now that same Spirit enables us to shape creation's beauty by skill and service, so that God's people may offer worship in spirit and in truth.

Prayer

Lord, help me to offer my gifts, to you and to others, as an act of thanksgiving for all that you have given.

JP

Responsible to the Spirit

The woman bore a son, and named him Samson. The boy grew, and the Lord blessed him. The spirit of the Lord began to stir in him in Mahaneh-dan, between Zorah and Eshtaol. Once Samson went down to Timnah, and at Timnah he saw a Philistine woman. Then he came up, and told his father and mother, 'I saw a Philistine woman at Timnah; now get her for me as my wife.'

Right through the Old Testament, God's Spirit often touches and equips people who have an important job to do. Yesterday we met the artists Bezalel and Oholiab. Samson is a colourful figure in quite another way. He was a heavyweight champion of his day, but was a strong character in more ways than one and Judges credits this to God's Spirit. From before his birth, he was called to 'deliver Israel from... the Philistines' (13:5). As he grew, God stirred in him. His strength was a gift and it was given for a purpose.

Yet, the first thing Samson does is fall for a Philistine girl. He seems not to notice that God's calling and this new relationship would tangle each other up, so that neither would ever be truly fulfilled. It's hard to carry on a love affair across a war zone, be a national hero when you're sleeping with the enemy or set up home when you're running raids on her people and property. By the end of his life, Samson was

a tragic figure—not quite wasted or worn out, but a shadow of what he might have become.

Maybe Samson is a warning. God gives rich gifts, but we do not always manage to use them well. The things we are drawn into, the people we become involved with, sometimes affect what we can do and be for God. Personal whims and wilfulness can get in the way of faithful service. The fact that we have the Holy Spirit in our lives may not always insulate us against the effects of our own mistakes. We need to be wise and careful, too. God's gift of the Holy Spirit is a responsibility, as well as a delight. 'Live by the Spirit,' says the Bible; 'do not grieve the Holy Spirit of God' (Galatians 5:16; Ephesians 4:30).

Prayer
Lord, help me to live wisely, so that your Spirit may work strongly through me.

JP

Root, shoot and fruit

A shoot shall come out from the stump of Jesse, and a branch shall grow out of his roots. The spirit of the Lord shall rest on him, the spirit of wisdom and understanding, the spirit of counsel and might, the spirit of knowledge and the fear of the Lord. His delight shall be in the fear of the Lord.

A number of Old Testament texts look longingly forward to God sending Israel a new leader. The writers yearned for someone—a prince, priest, prophet—who would live close to God and bring blessing and hope to God's people. Several of these texts appear in the early chapters of Isaiah and are taken up in the New Testament, where they are words about Jesus. This is one of them, which speaks of a coming king.

Jesse had been the father of David (1 Samuel 16) and David was remembered as a great king. Israel looked back in pride to his reign. If they could have another king like David, God would surely help them over their problems and fears. These verses, from three centuries after David's time, speak of a new shoot on an old tree stump, a new prince in an ancient royal line. The important thing about him would be God's Spirit. He would be a resourceful leader, rich in insight and faith, and these gifts would be from God.

'Wisdom and understanding' are about knowing God's world and its people truly and thoroughly. 'Counsel and might' mean working out the right thing to do and having the strength and energy to get it done. 'Knowledge and the fear of the Lord' are the faith and reverence that centre a person's life on God. According to this prophecy, the best God-given leadership will always be perceptive, practical and prayerful.

'His delight shall be in the fear of the Lord' is about putting God first and doing this gladly—these are signs that the Spirit is really at work within a person. Maybe Samson's problem (see yesterday's reading) was that he never really took delight in God. Isaiah's coming king would trust God, humbly and wholeheartedly. We must look forward through scripture to see who will fit this bill.

Prayer

God of the years, thank you for the good leaders you have given, in many areas of life. Guide those who lead our land and our churches.

JP

Spread of the Spirit

Then afterwards I will pour out my spirit on all flesh; your sons and your daughters shall prophesy, your old men shall dream dreams, and your young men shall see visions. Even on the male and female slaves, in those days, I will pour out my spirit. I will show portents in the heavens and on the earth, blood and fire and columns of smoke. The sun shall be turned to darkness, and the moon to blood, before the great and terrible day of the Lord comes. Then everyone who calls on the name of the Lord shall be saved.

Some of our Old Testament readings have spoken of God's Spirit breathing life into creation, yet only rarely does the Old Testament tell of the Spirit actually dwelling within men and women. There are some favoured individuals—leaders, prophets and so on—but this is not a widespread experience. It seems that the Spirit was for unusual people and special occasions only.

The prophet Joel knew that it would not always be this way. Maybe he was not sure himself as to how these hopes might be fulfilled, but he sensed that God had a wider purpose than his people had realized. The day would come when all sorts of people would be filled with the Spirit. Men and women, rich and poor, young and old—all would see with new eyes and speak confidently of God.

These words had an after-life. Centuries after Joel wrote them, Peter quoted them as he spoke to the crowds on the first Whitsun (Acts 2:16–21). 'This,' Peter said, 'is what Joel was writing about.' The Holy Spirit had come, in wind and fire and tongues. Pentecost meant Joel's words flew off the page and into the public square, off the horizon of hope and into history. Never again would the Spirit be a stranger to the world.

Christians believe that Joel's hopes are still being fulfilled as people around the world come to faith in Jesus. God is not restricted by race or rank or riches, nor by generation or gender. In every member of the body of Christ, 'God reveals the Spirit's presence, for the good of all' (1 Corinthians 12:7, my translation).

Prayer

Generous God, help me to rejoice when I see signs of your Spirit's presence in people around me.

JP

Sent to stay

And John testified, 'I saw the Spirit descending from heaven like a dove, and it remained on him. I myself did not know him, but the one who sent me to baptize with water said to me, "He on whom you see the Spirit descend and remain is the one who baptizes with the Holy Spirit." And I myself have seen and have testified that this is the Son of God.'

In John's Gospel, Jesus' baptism happens just off camera. We do not see Jesus in the water or coming up from it, but today's reading connects with accounts of his baptism in the other Gospels. John the Baptist was at work, down by the river. Jesus came to John and the Spirit came to Jesus.

'Descend and remain'—the words come twice, as if to stress the point. The Spirit had come to stay. The words of the Gospel echo a prophet's hopes, from long years before, that God's Spirit would 'rest' on a coming king (remember Tuesday's reading from Isaiah). Jesus would be the king Isaiah had longed for, a true prince in Israel, a beacon of hope for the people. He would understand God's ways and trust God truly.

'He is the one,' said the Baptist, 'who baptizes with the Holy Spirit.' Jesus had not received the Spirit for himself alone, but would share the Spirit readily and richly. As John immersed people in the Jordan, Jesus would release a river of God's presence and power into Israel, to flow across the land and flood lives with love. He would teach, heal and release people from evil. God's grace was at large and many lives would be refreshed and made whole by the Spirit's work.

When the Spirit rested on Jesus, then John knew that he was God's Son. In our day, God's Holy Spirit still helps many to recognize Jesus and trust him with their hopes. Realizing who Jesus is and coming to faith in him is not just something we work out for ourselves. Faith is a gift from God, stirred into life by the Spirit. It gives our lives a wholeness that we could never achieve or discover on our own.

Prayer

Lord Jesus Christ, help me to understand who you are, so that by your Spirit I may become the person I should be.

JP

Drink for the dry

On the last day of the festival, the great day, while Jesus was standing there, he cried out, 'Let anyone who is thirsty come to me, and let the one who believes in me drink. As the scripture has said, "Out of the believer's heart shall flow rivers of living water."' Now he said this about the Spirit, which believers in him were to receive; for as yet there was no Spirit, because Jesus was not yet glorified.

Here we see Jesus in Jerusalem, at the feast of Booths. At this festival, the people of Israel would remember the Exodus journey. They had lived in 'booths' along the way, which were makeshift shelters of leaves and branches. The festival recalled how God had helped them and brought them through the wilderness.

There were water-pouring ceremonies to remember the water God had given to keep the people alive, so, when Jesus spoke of himself as a source of living water, he was bringing this to life in a new way. 'It's in scripture,' he said and he was probably thinking of two sorts of Old Testament passage. Some (such as Psalm 78:15) looked back to the Exodus, to the water that burst from the rock in the desert. Other texts (like Ezekiel 47) looked forward and spoke of a river flowing from the Jerusalem temple, to moisten the dry earth. Now Jesus was taking these memories and hopes and connecting them to himself. He would refresh and sustain his people in the deserts of life and enable them to pass on his refreshment to others. He would be a source of new life, a place where heaven touched earth, renewing a thirsty world.

Yesterday we thought about Jesus 'baptizing with the Spirit', flooding the earth with God's goodness, but, during his ministry, the Spirit was tied to his person. The Spirit rested on Jesus, but had not yet been released by Jesus. Only when he was 'glorified'—crucified, risen and ascended—was the Spirit given more widely. Today's reading is about a promise held in suspense, prepared and inviting, but not quite ready to be fulfilled, which fits very well a couple of days before Whitsun itself.

Prayer

Lord Jesus, as you renew my living with your Spirit, help me to refresh people around me with a sense of your goodness and love.

JP

Scars of the Spirit

Jesus came and stood among them and said, 'Peace be with you.' After he said this, he showed them his hands and his side. Then the disciples rejoiced when they saw the Lord. Jesus said to them again, 'Peace be with you. As the Father has sent me, so I send you.' When he had said this, he breathed on them and said to them, 'Receive the Holy Spirit. If you forgive the sins of any, they are forgiven them; if you retain the sins of any, they are retained.'

The scene is Easter evening, with frightened disciples and locked doors. Suddenly Jesus appears and the mood changes. The sense of shock is transformed and tinged with gladness and glory. The world no longer seems lifeless and crushed: confidence and certainty can start to return.

This scene is a bridge between death and life, passion and Pentecost, Jesus' crucifixion and the coming of the Spirit. Jesus showed his friends his wounds, the marks left by nails and spear. He came to them as the Lamb bearing the marks of slaughter (Revelation 5:6). His body was scarred by the cross, as a sign of the love and pain of his dying, but he also breathed life into the room—a first instalment of the mighty wind of Whitsun and a promise of power to come. When the Spirit came, seven weeks afterwards, the disciples would know that this was sent by Jesus.

The Spirit would give Jesus' friends a big responsibility. It was to be their job to speak of both forgiveness and the demands of the gospel. They would help people to see the love that God offered and the commitment he asked. They would make known the message of the cross in their lives and words.

Whitsun is not a season when we leave the crucifixion behind, as if it had never been. Because Jesus died, we know the love of God and the Spirit makes this love real to the Church, as grace to live by and a goal to pursue. Pentecost is a time to celebrate the strength God gives and commit ourselves, again, as we follow the crucified and risen Jesus.

Prayer

Jesus, help us to celebrate in confidence, to serve in your strength and follow you without fear.

JP

Furnace of faith

When the day of Pentecost had come, they were all together in one place. And suddenly from heaven there came a sound like the rush of a violent wind, and it filled the entire house where they were sitting. Divided tongues, as of fire, appeared among them, and a tongue rested on each of them. All of them were filled with the Holy Spirit and began to speak in other languages, as the Spirit gave them ability.

The story of the first Whitsun is alarming and exciting, inviting and intimidating all at once. This was what Jesus had promised on Easter evening, and what his friends had been waiting for since his ascension, but they can scarcely have known quite what was coming. It seemed overwhelming and otherworldly, yet intimate and personal, too. They could not understand the power that had enfolded them, but they knew it was from God. Here were life and energy, from far beyond themselves, making God's presence truly part of them and one with them.

Wind and fire carry a hot draught, like a furnace where metal is hardened, purified and refined. The disciples were toughened and cleansed by this experience. Their faith became firm and sure in a way that it had not been before. They discovered new commitment, to God and to one another. They were more confident and convincing in what they said about Jesus. This was an intense and transforming moment, burning and blowing God's life into theirs.

As we look at it, it seems so strange... or so attractive. We get caught up in the detail and the drama. Some of us wish that it could happen to us, exactly as in Acts, and others are fearful, finding the incident scary and odd. Maybe attending too closely to the details, though, is a mistake. The main point is the gift, not the manner of the giving. God gave the Spirit for a purpose—to strengthen, sanctify, support and stir the Church. Whether we are attracted, alarmed or simply intrigued by wind and fire and tongues, God's Spirit can still meet each of us in a way that is right for us. God knows us well enough to deal with us in the way we need.

Prayer
Come, Holy Spirit. Renew my living.
As you know me, may I know you
more fully and more truly.

JP

God on Monday

Now during those days, when the disciples were increasing in number, the Hellenists complained against the Hebrews because their widows were being neglected in the daily distribution of food. And the twelve called together the whole community of the disciples and said, 'It is not right that we should neglect the word of God in order to wait on tables. Therefore, friends, select from among yourselves seven men of good standing, full of the Spirit and of wisdom, whom we may appoint to this task.'

This episode comes a little while after the first Whitsun. One of the first effects of the Spirit's coming was that Christians shared their goods and supported one another, acting as one body, a caring family. As they grew in number, though, this became more difficult. There were two language groups in the Church and one set of widows was overlooked.

You need practical people to tackle an issue like that—those with common sense, level heads, organization skills. That's what the apostles meant by 'full of wisdom', but they wanted people who were 'full of the Spirit', too. Our relationship with God affects how we relate to others. Trusting God helps to keep us trustworthy—which brings us to God on Monday.

The Bible talks often about a weekday sort of God. It can be easy to believe in the Holy Spirit on Sunday, if worship is good, Christian friends cheerful and kind and our faith gets a boost. The Holy Spirit, however, wants to come with us on Monday, too, and help us handle the practical tasks of the working week. Sharing out food, dealing with disgruntled people, trying to be fair, keeping an eye on accounts and stores and queues and quarrels—this was the need in Acts 6. This, too, was territory where the Spirit could help.

It can be the same with our Mondays, amid the headaches and hassles of the new week. Believing in the Holy Spirit may seem harder for us on Monday than on Sunday, but he will surely touch people this Monday, through your Christian service. Perhaps it will be in something as ordinary as doling out food.

Prayer

Thank you, Lord, that this is a day you have made. Help me to live by your Spirit in the duties and difficulties it brings.

JP

Stranger encounters

Now there was an Ethiopian eunuch, a court official of the Candace, queen of the Ethiopians, in charge of her entire treasury. He had come to Jerusalem to worship and was returning home; seated in his chariot, he was reading the prophet Isaiah. Then the Spirit said to Philip, 'Go over to this chariot and join it.' So Philip ran up to it and heard him reading the prophet Isaiah. He asked, 'Do you understand what you are reading?' He replied, 'How can I, unless someone guides me?'

This meeting on the road to Gaza arose because the Holy Spirit gave Philip a nudge. Philip was one of the 'seven men of good standing' in yesterday's reading who helped to organize the Church's support for widows. Later, he developed a ministry as a travelling preacher and here Acts shows him as a man of the Spirit, attuned to the prompting of God. He meets a high-ranking and thoughtful stranger.

The Ethiopian was well along the road, not only to Gaza, but also to faith. He was keen to worship and eager to learn of God. Travelling to Jerusalem and buying a biblical scroll would have taken a lot of time and money. Now he was reading, in Isaiah 53, about a man who suffered for the sake of others. 'Like a lamb, silent before its shearer' (Acts 8:32): who could this be?

The two men talked and Philip explained that Isaiah's words pointed to Jesus and to his suffer-ings and death. The Ethiopian understood, believed the good news and accepted baptism in a roadside pool. Then he travelled on, towards Egypt and the land we now call Sudan, as an ambassador for Christ, carrying the gospel deep into Africa.

There is no telling what the Spirit has in mind, if Christians are open to opportunities, strangers, needs and God. Only rarely do we meet someone with an open Bible, but surely many around us have open minds and hearts. Pray for such people, that God's Spirit will lead them to friends (or strangers) who can listen to their questions and help them along the road to faith. When we pray, though, we should also be ready, in case God wants to use us to answer that prayer.

Prayer

Lord, give me open eyes to see where your Spirit would lead me.

JP

Road blocks or building blocks?

[Paul, Silas and Timothy] went through the region of Phrygia and Galatia, having been forbidden by the Holy Spirit to speak the word in Asia. When they had come opposite Mysia, they attempted to go into Bithynia, but the Spirit of Jesus did not allow them; so, passing by Mysia, they went down to Troas. During the night Paul had a vision: there stood a man of Macedonia pleading with him and saying, 'Come over to Macedonia and help us.' When he had seen the vision, we immediately tried to cross over into Macedonia, being convinced that God had called us to proclaim the good news to them.

As we read Acts, we see the Holy Spirit often intervening at moments when the Church is on the threshold of something fresh. Perhaps a challenge lies ahead or the chance to speak about Jesus in a new setting. When there are frontiers to cross, for which human wisdom and courage do not suffice, God can prompt or push us, but, in this case, he seems to block the way, in a gradual process of guidance.

The eventual destination turns out to be Macedonia—northern Greece. By going there, Paul and his friends carried the Christian gospel into Europe. Although the ancients did not think of continents as we do (indeed, their 'Asia' was quite a small area, in western Turkey), this was still a big move, towards the heart of the Greek world. God's Spirit led them there, a step at a time.

When they started out, they could not see where the whole journey would take them. They must have fretted when their plans were barred at every turn. The Holy Spirit, so positive and purposeful at other times, now seemed to close every road. That is, until, as a gift rather than any human plan, came the summons to sail to Macedonia.

The wind of the Spirit can shut doors as well as open them and will often push us sideways rather than drive us forward. We may have to discover God's purposes gradually, even when we are busy about the work of the Church. If our plans are frustrated, this might be God's doing. If we can recognize this, even the roadblocks might help to build our faith.

Prayer

God of all wisdom, help me to recognize when to press on and when to change course.

JP

Daughters of Spirit

When we had finished the voyage from Tyre, we arrived at Ptolemais; and we greeted the believers and stayed with them for one day. The next day we left and came to Caesarea; and we went into the house of Philip the evangelist, one of the seven, and stayed with him. He had four unmarried daughters who had the gift of prophecy.

'Four unmarried daughters who prophesied'—the line could almost be taken from Jane Austen! Perhaps more was happening in this household than meets the eye. These 'prophet daughters' may have been rather like the 'sons of the prophets' in the Old Testament (see 2 Kings 6:1, for example). This would have been a little Christian training centre, where a seasoned church leader helped younger people grow in God's service.

Caesarea had been built in style and splendour by Herod the Great. It was also the seat of Roman imperial power in the Holy Land. Hardly, you might think, the most spiritual of places, yet here was a school of Christian prophecy, a company of godly women growing in faith and wisdom. The Holy Spirit was a major influence in Philip's life and he had had a varied and effective ministry. At this point he must have been a senior figure, encouraging others as they discovered the gifts of God's Spirit.

Later, this little company emigrated to the land we call Turkey. There the 'daughters' made a big impact and, for several generations to come, their memory was held in high honour by the Church, as recounted by the historian Eusebius. We do not know much about them, but, clearly, their lives and service counted. Joel's prophecy (27 May's reading) echoes across the years. Daughters prophesy, as well as sons; the young, as well as the old. The Spirit uses many different kinds of people, in important and lasting ways.

Whoever these 'daughters' were, their story has quite a message. The Holy Spirit is able to work in every generation; the old and the young need each other. When we value and nurture God's gifts, we may do long-term good. Never think you are too young or too old to respond to the Holy Spirit or for your life to count for Christ.

Reflection and prayer

Thank God for people older or younger than you, who have helped your Christian faith and life.

JP

Voice within

For all who are led by the Spirit of God are children of God. For you did not receive a spirit of slavery to fall back into fear, but you have received a spirit of adoption. When we cry, 'Abba! Father!' it is that very Spirit bearing witness with our spirit that we are children of God, and if children, then heirs, heirs of God and joint heirs with Christ—if, in fact, we suffer with him so that we may also be glorified with him.

Perhaps you remember the dreadful earthquake in China, just over a year ago. A little while after the disaster there was a snippet in the newspapers about a young woman who spent days walking round the ruins of the factory where her father worked. When others urged her to give up her search, that it was surely too late, she still went on calling, 'Father, father.' Eventually a weak voice answered from the rubble. Injured but alive, her father was pulled to safety.

In our own families, we know each other's voices often better than we know our own. We do not need to announce ourselves when we phone; the voice is enough. The care of family members can be a lifeline in a tough or tense situation, giving us the determination to go on.

Today's verses speak of the Holy Spirit as God's voice within us. When we pray to God as 'Father', the Spirit gives us the assurance that we have a right to do this. Our relationship with God is a gift and so is the confidence to live by it and enjoy it. We do not relate to God like slaves, living only by duty and command, but as children enfolded in love.

Belonging to God is a relationship of hope and the Spirit helps us look forward. We shall receive so much more than we experience at present. 'Heirs' are promised a full share of the family's wealth, the full measure of the eternal life of Jesus Christ. When we have to bear the pains and pressures of this earth, we listen to the voice that calls us children and we go on without fear.

Prayer
Pray for people you know who have much to bear and need patience and resilience for each day. Ask God to give them hope and courage.

JP

Known by God

Likewise the Spirit helps us in our weakness; for we do not know how to pray as we ought, but that very Spirit intercedes with sighs too deep for words. And God, who searches the heart, knows what is the mind of the Spirit, because the Spirit intercedes for the saints according to the will of God.

Many churches will celebrate tomorrow as Trinity Sunday and Christians will think together about God as Father, Son and Holy Spirit. Each one of the three persons of the Trinity is fully God, yet each has a different role and makes God known to us in a particular way. We have already read (last Sunday) about the Spirit as Jesus' gift to the Church. Today's reading tells of the Spirit as the Church's line of communication with God.

The Bible does not ask us to pretend that life is easy or straightforward. We live in a tangled and unhappy world and some of its sorrows flow around and through our own lives. The Holy Spirit does not remove us from these troubles, but we never face them alone. God is there, even when a situation is so painful that we can scarcely pray about it. It is hard to speak, even with God, about something really awful. Yet, even in the depths of confusion and distress, the Holy Spirit connects us gently and sensitively to the heart of God. Words will not meet the need, but words are not needed. God knows what we long for and understands all the burdens and cares that we carry.

The Spirit interprets us to God and interprets God within us. Heart to heart, there is an echo of belonging and love. We are understood. This pained world is known from within, not just because Jesus has been here, but because the Holy Spirit shares the care of God with the hurting places on earth. As friends of Jesus, as people of the Spirit, we are cared for and called to care, with the Spirit, for God's bruised and weary world.

Prayer

Lord, make me an instrument
of your peace;
where there is hatred,
let me sow love;
when there is injury, pardon;
where there is doubt, faith;
where there is despair, hope;
where there is darkness, light;
and where there is sadness, joy.

The prayer of St Francis

JP

Bible places: The city of Jerusalem

Welcome to Jerusalem! We are in the Middle East, 14 miles north-west of the Dead Sea and 33 miles east of the Mediterranean, ascending up to 2500 feet above sea level on the five hills that define the mile-and-a-half wide city. It is hot and barren here, especially in the summer months. In the late autumn, a sirocco wind sometimes blows from the south-eastern deserts, parching the land. Rain falls from October to May and, in February, it can be freezing, sometimes with snow.

For a few minutes of each day in the next two weeks, I invite you to travel with me to this ancient and wonderful city of Jerusalem, back to its very beginnings and from there through to the future. We will note the genesis of the Holy City in the Old Testament and our journey will finish in the revelation of the New Jerusalem in the Bible's closing pages. We shall visit ancient Israel and walk down the via dolorosa, along which Christ carried his cross.

Jerusalem has many names: Salem, Ariel (Isaiah 29), Moriah (where Abraham was called to sacrifice Isaac), the Holy City, the City of David, and Zion. The two Greek names for the city (both of which are used in the New Testament) are interesting. *Ierousalemi* is simply a transliteration of the Hebrew, but *Hierosolumai*, while similar, means something completely different. *Hieros* means 'holy', so, in Greek, Jerusalem is literally the 'Holy City'.

It is to this most holy of cities, significant at almost every stage of biblical history, that we now journey. As with any package tour, we cannot see everything and we will only be able to make brief stops as we travel in our biblical time machine, but our journey follows a thread that connects us to God, the ancient of days, who, in Christ, is the same yesterday, today and forever. Jerusalem, like any city, changes constantly and has seen more than its fair share of sorrow and pain, but it has also hosted sacred objects and witnessed divine events. Whether you have actually visited the Holy City, and thus have your own memories of Jerusalem, or have never done so, we travel now through the history of this fascinating and world-influencing place, not through space, but through time. Bon voyage!

Gordon Giles

Salem

After his return from the defeat of Chedorlaomer and the kings who were with him, the king of Sodom went out to meet [Abram] at the Valley of Shaveh (that is, the King's Valley). And King Melchizedek of Salem brought out bread and wine; he was priest of God Most High. He blessed him and said, 'Blessed be Abram by God Most High, maker of heaven and earth; and blessed be God Most High, who has delivered your enemies into your hand!' And Abram gave him one tenth of everything.

This is the first biblical reference to Jerusalem, the spiritual home of Judaism. In the 19th century BC, the Egyptians called it Urusalimum. A Semitic (Hebrew) variation on this, Urusalim, can be traced to Tel al Armana in the 14th century BC. The Assyrian King Sennacherib called it Ursalimmu in the seventh century BC and, although he tried to capture it, he never succeeded (see 2 Kings 19:15–34). These original names have two roots—'Uru' meaning 'city' and 'Salim', a name for a god. Thus Jerusalem has always been known as a city of a god, but it is not the God of the Hebrews, the God of Abraham and Isaac and of Jesus Christ, after whom it is named. Salim was an Amorite god, whose name lives on in the Jerusalem of today.

Yet it is Abraham (Abram), revered as a founding father in the three religions that hold Jerusalem dear—Christianity, Judaism and Islam—with whom Jerusalem is first associated in Genesis. Further, Melchizedek, the archetypal first high priest of the one and only God, greets him there, offering him bread and wine in a gesture of friendship and fellowship.

Abram's nephew, Lot, was captured in a battle near the Dead Sea, so Abram attacked Chedorlaomer's invaders and restored order. The priest Melchizedek thanked him, recognizing that Abram was also a worshipper of the singular creator God. Abram responded with a tithe, 'one tenth of everything'. The writer of Hebrews quotes this passage in 7:1–2, relating Jesus to a priestly succession that goes right back to Abraham and Melchizedek's encounter on a spot that became pivotal in world history.

Reflection

The faith we share today connects us to ancient places at the dawn of history.

GG

City of David

> The king and his men marched to Jerusalem against the Jebusites, the inhabitants of the land, who said to David, 'You will not come in here, even the blind and the lame will turn you back'—thinking, 'David cannot come in here.' Nevertheless David took the stronghold of Zion, which is now the city of David... David occupied the stronghold, and named it the city of David. David built the city all around from the Millo inwards.

Particular places can have meaning for us, whether they are large spaces, cities, specific buildings or even rooms. We hold dear the places where the significant events in our lives took place: where marriage was proposed, weddings occurred, holidays were enjoyed or battles fought. Something of ourselves remains in these places and they connect us to moments of joy or pain. They can be vivid in our minds when they are far away and, when we return to them, there is a real sense of homecoming, even if those locations are not in fact 'home' in the strict sense of the word. Such places can be cathedrals, mountains, alleyways or sports stadia. For Christians who have been there, Jerusalem can be such a place, due to its centrality in the story of the events that shaped Jesus' life and ministry. Jerusalem is the place of crucifixion and resurrection.

This sense of place—of 'sacred space'—is very important to Jews, whose history is to some extent one that involves places, with Jerusalem being very much a focal point. When the Israelites settled there after the wilderness period (40 years after the Exodus from Egypt), the local people were the Jebusites —one of various tribes known as Canaanites. The city of Jebus lay on the boundary between the lands of the tribes of Judah and Benjamin (see Joshua 18:15–17). A land ridge, running south of where the temple was later built, was known locally as Zion. When David captured the city of Jebus, it soon became known as the 'City of David' and the name 'Zion' took on a spiritual and nationalistic significance that retains its potency, especially for those who feel particularly connected to the city of Jerusalem as the central location of their faith.

Prayer

Thank you, Lord, for the places that help us connect with each other and with you. Amen

GG

1 KINGS 6:1–2, 38 (NRSV)

Solomon's temple

In the four hundred and eightieth year after the Israelites came out of the land of Egypt, in the fourth year of Solomon's reign over Israel, in the month of Ziv, which is the second month, he began to build the house of the Lord. The house that King Solomon built for the Lord was sixty cubits long, twenty cubits wide, and thirty cubits high… In the eleventh year, in the month of Bul, which is the eighth month, the house was finished in all its parts, and according to all its specifications. He was seven years in building it.

While it was King David who purchased and prepared the ground for building the first temple, it was his successor, Solomon, who actually oversaw the construction between 959 and 952 BC. It was evidently a priority, as he began it early in his reign and it took seven years (while, interestingly, his palace took 13 years to build). Thus Salem, or Zion, the City of David, became the central location of the Jewish faith, with the resting place of the tabernacle located in the temple there. What a place it was, too! The description in 1 Kings 6 is worth reading in full and wondering at: gold everywhere and beautiful woodcarvings adorned one of the wonders of the world.

Sadly this temple was first ransacked by the Babylonians in 597BC and then destroyed. A second temple was begun around 538BC and completed just over 20 years later (see Ezra 5:1—6:18). It survived the Roman invasion led by Pompey in 63BC (he entered but did not damage it), but when Herod became a Roman puppet ruler in 37BC, he devised a bigger and better temple, which was not fully completed until AD64. The Romans destroyed it during their suppression of rebellion in AD70 and now all that remains is the Wailing Wall, at which Jews and others pray and lament not only the lack of a complete temple but also the strife in the world. Thus, while the holy city of Jerusalem is held dear by Jews, Christians and Muslims alike, its history makes it a place of both sorrow and hope.

Prayer

Lord, thank you that you are not bound by location. Build in our hearts temples of faith, hope and love. Amen

GG

Jerusalem's peace prayer

I was glad when they said to me, 'Let us go to the house of the Lord!' Our feet are standing within your gates, O Jerusalem. Jerusalem—built as a city that is bound firmly together. To it the tribes go up, the tribes of the Lord, as was decreed for Israel, to give thanks to the name of the Lord. For there the thrones for judgment were set up, the thrones of the house of David. Pray for the peace of Jerusalem: 'May they prosper who love you. Peace be within your walls, and security within your towers.'

It was quite a way to begin a wedding! My wife and I chose this psalm, set to music by C.H.H. Parry, as the piece to which she walked down the aisle of St Paul's Cathedral in September 2000. The previous woman to do so had been Diana, Princess of Wales, in 1982. Just as that piece of music is special to us, so too is that place and for us the two are linked. Perhaps for you, too, certain pieces of music carry you to certain places, which themselves connect you to a part of your life. That is how both music and places can acquire spiritual significance.

It can work for nations, too. For many, St Paul's Cathedral is forever associated with that royal wedding and Westminster Abbey with a sad funeral 16 years later. Back in Jerusalem, the temple was even more significant, as a place of rejoicing and blessing. This 'Song of Ascents' was literally that—a song to be sung as pilgrims climbed the mount of Moriah where the temple stood. To do so was an occasion of joy and achievement as some had travelled many miles. They celebrated the firm foundation of the holy city where they had come to worship and they came to pray for the prosperity and peace of their spiritual capital.

Jerusalem is still a place of pilgrimage and, as such, has been fought over—notably during the several crusades that took place during the Middle Ages. Pilgrimage, politics and conflict still characterize Jerusalem. Is Jerusalem in the news today? It could well be. This psalm is just as relevant now as it was during the time of Solomon's temple.

Prayer

*Lord, we pray for peace in Jerusalem and elsewhere, this and every day.
Amen*

GG

51

Jerusalem's new song

Arise, shine; for your light has come, and the glory of the Lord has risen upon you... Foreigners shall build up your walls, and their kings shall minister to you; for in my wrath I struck you down, but in my favour I have had mercy on you. Your gates shall always be open; day and night they shall not be shut, so that nations shall bring you their wealth, with their kings led in procession... they shall call you the City of the Lord, the Zion of the Holy One of Israel... I will appoint Peace as your overseer and Righteousness as your taskmaster... you shall call your walls Salvation, and your gates Praise.

Jerusalem has had a chequered history, encompassing ancient culture, destruction, rejuvenation and, as here, a visionary hope for future security and peace. While the book of Revelation extends this vision to include the risen Christ, Isaiah's description still inspires. It comes as the hope of restoration after a series of assaults that began after Solomon's death. The monarchy was divided, weakening Jerusalem militarily, and the Egyptians were the first to attack for financial gain (2 Chronicles 12:9). The army of Aram then looted the temple (24:23–24) and, later, the king of Israel (a separate monarchy now) broke down part of Jerusalem's north wall. Rezin of Syria and Pekah of Israel jointly attacked Ahaz, who tried to do a deal with the Assyrians (see 2 Kings 16:1–7). This backfired, costing Jerusalem a fortune to avoid destruction. Around 701BC, the Assyrian Sennacherib invaded,

troubling the Babylonians, who therefore assisted Jerusalem, but the alliance failed to oust the Assyrians (see Isaiah 36—39). From Isaiah's perspective, these were instances of God punishing an impious, morally degenerate city.

Isaiah, however, foresaw a revived, new Jerusalem, unhindered by war and tribute tax to other powers. In a sense, this came about while the Assyrians were preoccupied with a Babylonian threat and King Josiah reigned (639–609BC). The temple reopened and a copy of the law of Moses was discovered. Jerusalem experienced a relatively rare period of religious revival, during which the Passover was reinstated (2 Kings 23:21).

Prayer

Lord, things seem never to change: bring peace to the Middle East and renew your people there. Amen

GG

52

JEREMIAH 7:30–34 (NRSV, ABRIDGED)

Jerusalem wasted

The people of Judah have done evil in my sight, says the Lord; they have set their abominations in the house that is called by my name, defiling it. And they go on building the high place of Topheth, which is in the valley of the son of Hinnom, to burn their sons and their daughters in the fire... Therefore, the days are surely coming, says the Lord, when it will no more be called Topheth... but the valley of Slaughter... The corpses of this people will be food for the birds of the air, and for the animals of the earth; and no one will frighten them away. And I will bring to an end the sound of mirth and gladness... in the cities of Judah and in the streets of Jerusalem; for the land shall become a waste.

During Jerusalem's relatively peaceful period under Josiah, a prophet called Jeremiah spoke freely and had the ear of those in power. Meanwhile, Babylon gained strength at Assyria's expense—first under Nabopolassar and then his son Nebuchadnezzar. In 610BC, Pharaoh Neco went to Assyria's aid, marching through Judah without permission, and Josiah attacked his troops. This was a mistake: Josiah was mortally injured.

Jeremiah had already begun to see warning signs of a Babylonian invasion and had plenty of reason to suppose that God would allow such a thing. This passage sets out a theme to which Jeremiah returns repeatedly. Jerusalem and surrounding Judah, he said, had turned away from God to Baal and Baalist sacrifices. So God's punishment would be meted out by the Babylonians, who would lay the city waste and exile its people. No one wanted to hear this, of course, and it got Jeremiah into a lot of trouble, even though he was proved right.

Jeremiah also preached against alliances with Egypt, which, because of their victories against Nebuchadnezzar, gained the prophet even more enemies, including King Jehoiakim, son of Josiah. He was killed in 599BC, as Jeremiah had predicted (22:19), and the new 18-year-old king, Jehoiachin, surrendered in 597BC and, with 18,000 others (the prophet Ezekiel among them), was carted off to Babylon (see 2 Kings 24:8–12).

Prayer

Lord, here we have no abiding city, but turn to you for the hope of one to come. Amen

GG

Zion remembered

By the rivers of Babylon—there we sat down and there we wept when we remembered Zion. On the willows there we hung up our harps. For there our captors asked us for songs, and our tormentors asked for mirth, saying, 'Sing us one of the songs of Zion!' How could we sing the Lord's song in a foreign land? If I forget you, O Jerusalem, let my right hand wither! Let my tongue cling to the roof of my mouth, if I do not remember you, if I do not set Jerusalem above my highest joy.

When the Babylonians exiled many of Jerusalem's inhabitants, and the city was destroyed in 587BC, the people were not only humiliated but they also became like orphans. Jerusalem was not only home; it was the location of the temple and the temple was the dwelling place of God (Psalm 76:2). It is hard for us to appreciate this for, while there are buildings that are important in our national and religious life, we do not maintain one of them is God's sole dwelling.

Jesus told the Samaritan woman at Jacob's well (John 4:20–21) that God would no longer be worshipped only on Mount Zion. God has many dwelling places, particularly in our hearts, where his Spirit dwells. The exiles in Babylon did not see it that way and being deprived of the right to live in or even visit Jerusalem was a massive blow. Yet, they understood that music and place can be linked and singing the songs of Zion (strictly Psalms 46, 48, 76, 84, 87 and 122) out of context stirred painful memories of not only the loss of their homes but also God's abandonment of them. They needed to remember Jerusalem, but singing songs that reminded them of past happiness was too hard—so hard, in fact, all they could do was weep.

I wonder if there are songs that make you sad. They might do so because they remind you of happy times long gone or because they recall a sad event, such as a death. For the people in Babylonian exile, the songs of Zion did both as Jerusalem memories evoked the best of times and the worst of times.

Prayer

Lord, you are everywhere. May the joyful music of your love always find a place in our hearts. Amen

GG

The second temple

'Thus says King Cyrus of Persia: The Lord, the God of heaven, has given me all the kingdoms of the earth, and he has charged me to build him a house at Jerusalem in Judah. Any of those among you who are of his people—may their God be with them!—are now permitted to go up to Jerusalem in Judah, and rebuild the house of the Lord, the God of Israel—he is the God who is in Jerusalem; and let all survivors, in whatever place they reside, be assisted by the people of their place with silver and gold, with goods and with animals, besides freewill offerings for the house of God in Jerusalem.'

In 536BC King Cyrus, having defeated the Babylonians, allowed Sheshbazzar, Prince of Judah, to return and begin the rebuilding of the city and temple. The governor, Zerubbabel, and the high priest Jeshua prepared to start work on the temple, but it was only after Darius became king of Babylon and with the encouragement of the prophets Haggai and Zechariah (Ezra 4:24—5:2) that work began in earnest. After four years, the temple was ready for use (but not completely rebuilt by any means) and worship in the holy city resumed. It had been 70 years since the destruction of the first temple, as Jeremiah had predicted (Jeremiah 25:11).

The writer Ezra was not part of this advance party. He returned to Jerusalem 30 years later (around 458BC; see Ezra 7:7). Although operational, the rebuilt temple was in a sorry state, still with broken walls, and Ezra's party brought gold and silver with which to decorate it. It was not until Nehemiah arrived in 444BC that things really got going in the city as a whole. Ezra himself was a scribe and a priest, a man well-versed in scripture, law and theology, and, unlike the 'scribes' of Jesus' time, he was a religious leader in his own right who could trace his priestly lineage back to King David. His reforms of the temple and Jewish life and worship are often forgotten now, but it was his piety and vision that renewed Jerusalem's status.

Prayer

By his mercy, the Lord casts down the mighty and raises up the fallen. Blessed be his holy name. Amen

GG

Jerusalem rebuilt

I went out by night by the Valley Gate past the Dragon's Spring and to the Dung Gate, and I inspected the walls of Jerusalem that had been broken down and its gates that had been destroyed by fire. Then I went on to the Fountain Gate and to the King's Pool; but there was no place for the animal I was riding to continue. So I went up by way of the valley by night and inspected the wall. Then I turned back... I had not yet told the Jews, the priests, the nobles, the officials, and the rest that were to do the work. Then I said to them, 'You see the trouble we are in, how Jerusalem lies in ruins... Come, let us rebuild the wall of Jerusalem, so that we may no longer suffer disgrace.'

For the first time in history, more than half of the world's population now live in cities; in 1900 only 13 per cent lived in urban conurbations. While it has taken thousands of years, cities have become places people aspire to live in and history illustrates the slow, steady process of urbanization.

In Nehemiah's description of the ruins of Jerusalem, we gain a sense of the mammoth task that lay ahead of those who sought to rebuild the city. While Ezra was particularly concerned with rebuilding the temple and restoring worship, Nehemiah had the wider task of reconstructing a ruined urban environment. (Originally, the books of Ezra and Nehemiah were joined together—they were only separated by the theologian Origen in the third century AD.) Nehemiah was a cupbearer in Babylon, who secretly inspected the ruined city and enlisted those who had returned with Zerubbabel to rebuild. It was a dangerous project as the neighbouring tribes objected and the builders had to be prepared to defend themselves. Nevertheless, rebuilding the walls took only 52 days and then people began to move in and settle, as we read in the later chapters of Nehemiah.

Nehemiah was a strong, faithful character who has inspired many in the cause of reformation and restoration. His vigour shows us that, even today, under God, progress can be made against all odds in various walks of life, whether we live in a city or the countryside.

Prayer

Father God, with Christ as our guide and helper, we cannot fail. Amen

GG

Jerusalem Passover

The Passover of the Jews was near, and Jesus went up to Jerusalem. In the temple he found people selling cattle, sheep, and doves, and the money changers seated at their tables. Making a whip of cords, he drove all of them out of the temple... The Jews then said to him, 'What sign can you show us for doing this?' Jesus answered them, 'Destroy this temple, and in three days I will raise it up.'... When he was in Jerusalem during the Passover festival, many believed in his name because they saw the signs that he was doing.

Jesus, like other Jews of his time, was in the habit of going to Jerusalem for the Passover festival (see John 11:55). In fact, it is still traditional for Jews to celebrate Passover in Jerusalem at least once in their lives. While Jerusalem was not the location of the first Passover, which immediately preceded the Exodus from Egypt (see Exodus 12), it became the 'spiritual home' of the Passover and the festival of Unleavened Bread, which follows it. Thus, Jesus was accustomed to going to Jerusalem from an early age: the occasion when, aged 12, he became separated from Mary and Joseph was at the end of such a visit (see Luke 2:41).

Since the destruction of the temple in Jerusalem in AD 70, the Jewish Passover no longer includes lamb meat, but a shank bone is placed on the table. In Jesus' time, however, the Passover lamb was very significant, as food and as a symbol of God's providence and of messianic hope. The temple priests had a monopoly on supplying 'unblemished' lambs for Passover meals, and it was this unfair practice that Jesus criticized when, literally, he turned the tables on them. His reply, referring to himself, 'Destroy this temple, and... I will raise it up', is doubly prophetic as he associates himself with both the Passover lamb and the temple itself, the site of worship, the holiness of which will be effectively transferred to Jesus himself, the crucified, risen, ascended saviour. Such actions and associations were politically powerful, religious dynamite, the repercussions of which still reverberate today.

Prayer

Christ, our Passover, you have been sacrificed for us. May we celebrate you in bread and wine. Amen

GG

King of Jerusalem?

The next day the great crowd that had come to the festival heard that Jesus was coming to Jerusalem. So they took branches of palm trees and went out to meet him, shouting, 'Hosanna! Blessed is the one who comes in the name of the Lord—the King of Israel!' Jesus found a young donkey and sat on it; as it is written: 'Do not be afraid, daughter of Zion. Look, your king is coming, sitting on a donkey's colt!'

This upbeat event, from which we derive Palm Sunday celebrations, is not often seen as a scene of temptation, yet the crowd yielded to the temptation to hail Jesus as a revolutionary, Roman-overthrowing king. The people can hardly be blamed—after all, Jesus did ride on a donkey, fulfilling the prophecy of Zechariah 9:9. It was a deliberate act, designed to resonate with prophecy. It also throws Jesus back to that moment at the beginning of his ministry, when, tempted by Satan, he was taken from the wilderness to Jerusalem, placed on top of the temple and taunted: 'If you are the Son of God, throw yourself down from here, for it is written, "He will command his angels concerning you, to protect you"' (Luke 4:9–10).

Jerusalem, as the seat of temporal and spiritual power, had a lure, even for Jesus, who had to resist the temptation to be what others wanted him to be: a showy, military leader. This must have been particularly hard as he entered what he knew would be a difficult, painful, fatal few days. Riding on that colt, the temptation to go with the flow must have been strong and he might have recalled the scene in the wilderness three years earlier, when he overcame Satan's offer of invincibility and power. Here that testing offer was being made real.

Jesus' call to suffering servanthood and his resistance to the offer of a rebellious kingship is unique in history, yet the call to be ourselves and fulfil our true vocation in the face of temptation is universal. We may not be called to high office or revolutionary leadership, but we are all monarchs of our own integrity and, with the Spirit's help, we submit to none other than Christ to rule our lives.

Prayer

Christ, our servant King, you are our God: we offer you our lives. Amen

GG

Jerusalem's desolation

[Jesus said] 'When you see Jerusalem surrounded by armies, then know that its desolation has come near. Then those in Judea must flee to the mountains, and those inside the city must leave it, and those out in the country must not enter it; for these are days of vengeance, as a fulfilment of all that is written. Woe to those who are pregnant and to those who are nursing infants in those days! For there will be great distress on the earth and wrath against this people; they will fall by the edge of the sword and be taken away as captives among all nations; and Jerusalem will be trampled on by the Gentiles.'

Even though Jesus never saw the completed temple, these words are an accurate description of what happened between AD66 and 70. After Pentecost, Jesus' followers remained in Jerusalem, where they were visited by Paul (Acts 15). They endured famine, for which they received help from Macedonian Christians (Romans 15:25–26). Within two years of the completion of Herod's temple in AD64, there was an uprising, however, and the Christians fled to the city of Pella, east of the Jordan. The Romans failed to quell the revolt and, in AD70, they attacked the city's north wall without success. Then they besieged the city, causing starvation inside. After finally scaling the wall of the fortress of Antonia, the troops wreaked havoc, killing or enslaving the weakened inhabitants and razing the temple to the ground, with the exception of three towers and the part of the western wall that remains and is now called the Wailing Wall.

Given the importance of the temple, the thought that (once again) it would be destroyed was a desolate one for Jesus' hearers. It would be interpreted as a judgment, as the destruction of the first temple by the Babylonians had been. Rome and Babylon had much in common from a Jewish perspective. National pride would be crushed; indeed the very completion of the temple may have sparked fervour in the first place. Once Jerusalem had a new temple, it may have inspired the rebels to launch a disastrous uprising. It seems that Jesus saw it all coming.

Prayer

Lord, hear our prayer for those who endure the violent destruction of their homes and lives today. Amen

GG

Jerusalem Council

Certain individuals came down from Judea and were teaching the brothers, 'Unless you are circumcised according to the custom of Moses, you cannot be saved.' And after Paul and Barnabas had no small dissension and debate with them, Paul and Barnabas and some of the others were appointed to go up to Jerusalem to discuss this question with the apostles and the elders... When they came to Jerusalem, they were welcomed by the church... and they reported all that God had done with them. But some believers... stood up and said, 'It is necessary for them to be circumcised and ordered to keep the law of Moses.' The apostles and the elders met together to consider this matter. After there had been much debate, Peter stood up and said to them, '... We believe that we will be saved through the grace of the Lord Jesus, just as they will.'

What must I do to be saved? This was the question under consideration as Paul travelled to Jerusalem to meet with the apostles who had walked with Jesus himself. Jerusalem, the site of Christ's passion, is once again the heart of a burgeoning religion and Paul has some ideas about salvation that must be tested against the memories and understanding of the pillars of the Church—Peter among them. They are the men who hold authority in the place of power, Jerusalem. It was the city of the temple, where the Jewish priesthood was based, the city where God chose to reveal himself in Christ to die for the world.

When we read the New Testament we soon conclude that Christ's saving work is universal. Around AD49, when this meeting took place, the Gospels were not in print and decisions had to be reached as to whether or not Paul and Barnabas should take Christ's message to those whom the Jews had traditionally excluded. This is where the early Church comes to understand what it is and whom it is for. In spite of the Judaizers who provoke this debate, arguing that Christians should convert to Judaism first, the Jerusalem Council decided to let Paul continue preaching to the Gentiles and, because he did so, you are reading this now.

Prayer

Jesus we praise you for the wisdom, courage and grace of those to whom you entrusted your gospel of salvation. Amen

GG

New Jerusalem

I saw a new heaven and a new earth; for the first heaven and the first earth had passed away, and the sea was no more. And I saw the holy city, the new Jerusalem, coming down out of heaven from God, prepared as a bride adorned for her husband... And in the spirit [the angel] carried me away to a great, high mountain and showed me the holy city Jerusalem coming down out of heaven from God... I saw no temple in the city, for its temple is the Lord God the Almighty and the Lamb.

This is our ultimate destination on our Jerusalem time tour. We now stand in the future: the world has ended, tribulation is over and ecological or cosmological catastrophe has passed. Now the old city of God has been transformed and a 'new' Jerusalem is inaugurated, as an embodiment of human hope for an eternal dwelling place in the presence of God. It is a truly glorious place, with jasper walls, pearly gates and streets of gold. The tree of life grows there and, through it, flows the river of life. It needs no sun or moon, there is no distinction between day and night, and there is no temple. We may be able to picture these wonders, but there is a deeper meaning, too.

In the Old Testament, the temple represented the aspirations of the nation and the presence of God. The prophets saw Jerusalem decline as people sinned, but Isaiah and Ezekiel had visions of reconstruction. John's vision is the culmination of a tradition of divinely assisted rise and fall and rebirth, to which Jesus himself refers when predicting the fate of Jerusalem (see Mark 13:1–2, 26).

In Greek, there are two words that we translate as 'new': when a city is rebuilt, it is new. Here, though, John sees a 'new' Jerusalem that is clean and pure, cleansed and different, heralding a new order. The same sense is found in the 'new' attached to testament, covenant and creation. In fact, it is Christ, Son of God and redeemer of the world, who is the new Jerusalem, in whom all things are made new (Revelation 21:5), and the history of Jerusalem is, in a sense, the story of salvation.

Prayer

Lord, as we have journeyed through the history of Jerusalem, renew us on our pilgrimage until we reach the heavenly new Jerusalem. Amen.

GG

2 Samuel 8—15

If you enjoy soap operas, you're going to enjoy the next two weeks. These chapters contain violence, cruelty, murder, adultery, incest, rape, betrayal and treason. So—just the kind of material with which to start the day! Actually, that's not so far from the truth. If the Bible only dealt with 'nice' people and pleasant outcomes, it would be fiction. Instead, it is a 'biography' with much to teach us.

First, though, we need to locate David in history. He lived just after 1000BC, which, in that region, makes him an Iron Age king. As such, he was a man of his time, though some of his values may shock us today. We should, however, be careful about making any judgments. If history teaches us anything, it's that each generation has a habit of criticizing the sins of previous generations while ignoring its own. If our culture is without sin, it is justifiable to throw stones at David's. If not, then we should trust David and ourselves to the judgment of God.

David's world was made up of warring kings and, when we read about the battles, injury and death, we may be sickened. We do need to understand how they counted at this time, though. In their non-technical world, precision was not required, so counting tended to go like this: 1, 2, 3 (and so forth up to around 10), then straight on to 15, 20, 50 and then to, oh, hundreds, followed by… thousands! So their 'fifteen thousand' if counted in a contemporary way might actually be nearer to fifteen hundred. It's good to keep this in mind when we read about the battles and try to make sense of the numbers of soldiers involved and the appalling death tolls recorded.

These chapters may be a challenge if we have been given a 'Sunday school' version of David's life (heavily edited, with the positives emphasized and the negatives left out). These chapters tell of the real David, in both public and private life. On many occasions, he is found wanting and we may be tempted to lose patience with him and, perhaps, with the Old Testament. The truth, though, is this: although David was a man of his time, he was a man of God—and God chose him in spite of his cultural baggage. In other words, even though 3000 years separate us, he was just like us.

David Robertson

Victories

David defeated the Philistines and subdued them, and he took Metheg Ammah from the control of the Philistines... David fought Hadadezer son of Rehob, king of Zobah, when he went to restore his control along the Euphrates River... When the Arameans of Damascus came to help Hadadezer king of Zobah, David struck down twenty-two thousand of them. He put garrisons in the Aramean king- dom of Damascus, and the Arameans became subject to him and brought tribute. The Lord gave David victory wherever he went... And David became famous after he returned from striking down eighteen thousand Edomites in the Valley of Salt. He put garrisons throughout Edom, and all the Edomites became subject to David... David reigned over all Israel, doing what was just and right for all his people.

Today's reading is an edited version, leaving out the full toll of death and violence. We're not pretending that the violence isn't there; it's so that we can focus on the main issue: did the Lord give David the victory, as verse 14 says? David evidently thought so, as did his neighbours and the historian who wrote these accounts.

This issue can leave today's Christians confused. We are comfortable with the idea that God's people were protected from neighbouring marauders and David was a just king, but uncomfortable that this was achieved through violence and cruelty. So, what's going on?

In biblical terms, David was being a good shepherd. Part of the shepherd's task was to protect the flock from bears and lions—that's why he carried weapons. David the shepherd boy was no stranger to combat (1 Samuel 17:34–37) and, when he became king, he was just as ready to fight human predators who threatened his new 'flock'— the people of Israel. In the same way, God was shepherding his people by giving David the victory.

For David (and for Christians in the world today), there was (and is) a physical aspect to shepherding. In our own culture, we are used to thinking of 'shepherds' in spiritual terms, but, even here, when the 'shepherds' care for the 'sheep', they may need practical strategies to deal with 'bears and lions'.

Prayer

Lord, give our shepherds discernment and strength.

DR

A vow completed

David asked, 'Is there anyone still left of the house of Saul to whom I can show kindness for Jonathan's sake?'... When Mephibosheth son of Jonathan, the son of Saul, came to David, he bowed down to pay him honour... 'Don't be afraid,' David said to him, 'for I will surely show you kindness for the sake of your father Jonathan. I will restore to you all the land that belonged to your grandfather Saul, and you will always eat at my table.' Mephibosheth bowed down and said, 'What is your servant, that you should notice a dead dog like me?'... And Mephibosheth lived in Jerusalem, because he always ate at the king's table, and he was crippled in both feet.

Poor Mephibosheth. He was Jonathan's son and therefore next in line to the throne, except that the kingdom had now passed to David and his descendants. Mephibosheth had good reason to fear David: just by being alive he was a threat and, if the king noticed him, he might not live for very long. To add to his problems, his grandfather, Saul, had made many enemies (see 2 Samuel 21:1–14) and, to make his life even more difficult, he was crippled in both feet. Mephibosheth, then, was sensibly keeping a low profile.

David had other ideas. He wanted to honour his friend Jonathan and was secure enough in his anointing to ignore Mephibosheth's claim to the throne. He restored Saul's farmland to him, gave him servants to work it and welcomed him to the royal court. For Mephibosheth it must have been a wonderful, unexpected outcome.

Now, what does that remind us of? Nearly a thousand years later, the 'son of David' invited the lowest of the low to join his royal court—and he still does. For Christians down the ages and across the world, being invited to dwell in the presence of the King of kings is a wonderful, unexpected outcome from meeting Jesus.

The story doesn't end there. As Christians, we are called to continue this work of God's Spirit— the work of welcome. David and Jesus shared the same Spirit (1 Samuel 16:13; Mark 1:10) and so do we. For us, the question is this: 'Is there anyone to whom I can show kindness for Jesus' sake?'

Prayer

Lord, thank you for inviting even me to your table.

DR

More battles

When David was told of [the Aramean army], he gathered all Israel, crossed the Jordan and went to Helam. The Arameans formed their battle lines to meet David and fought against him. But they fled before Israel, and David killed seven hundred of their charioteers and forty thousand of their foot soldiers. He also struck down Shobach the commander of their army, and he died there. When all the kings who were vassals of Hadadezer saw that they had been defeated by Israel, they made peace with the Israelites and became subject to them. So the Arameans were afraid to help the Ammonites any more.

It's worth reminding ourselves that these were not wars as we would recognize them. The Israelites would have fought the Arameans in a 'one day event', with each army squaring up to the other across the field of battle, charging, fighting and winning or losing. It's probably also true that these 'wars' entailed fewer overall casualties than contemporary wars, which range across vast territories for months, years and even decades.

They were still wars, though, and, at any time, the king could lose and then everything would change as a new king would take possession of the people. It's hardly surprising that Psalm 3 is not the only psalm to cry for God's help to overcome so many foes. This must have been the constant prayer of God's people in David's time, just as it has been down the centuries. In the Church of England, the form for daily prayers still asks God to defend his people 'from the fear of their enemies that they may pass their time in rest and quietness'. In times of uncertainty, prayers for peace are highly significant.

What of our own prayers? We live in a world where war is constant, violence is before us in every news bulletin and more than a few of us live in communities threatened by hostility. We pray for nations, victims, reconciliation, peace and protection and these prayers make our time not so very different from David's. Perhaps we might also pray for those military leaders who, like David, seek to ensure the safety of ordinary people, even when the choices they have to make are hard and the cost in casualties may be high.

Prayer
Defend us, O Lord, that we may live in peace.

DR

2 SAMUEL 11:1–4 (NIV, ABRIDGED)

Temptation

In the spring, at the time when kings go off to war, David sent Joab out with the king's men and the whole Israelite army. They destroyed the Ammonites and besieged Rabbah. But David remained in Jerusalem. One evening David got up from his bed and walked around on the roof of the palace. From the roof he saw a woman bathing. The woman was very beautiful, and David sent someone to find out about her. The man said, 'Isn't this Bathsheba, the daughter of Eliam and the wife of Uriah the Hittite?' Then David sent messengers to get her. She came to him, and he slept with her... Then she went back home.

The wars continue, but David is not leading the charge. He is on the roof of his palace, enjoying a cool, spring evening. Then he stumbles on a sight not meant for his eyes and is tempted. Usually, we regard temptation as a 'whirlwind' that overcomes and defeats us in an instant. In reality, temptation is often a slow process with choices presenting themselves along the way and, here, David takes four deliberate steps towards his goal.

His first step is that he watches Bathsheba. He could have turned away, but he didn't. David's second step was to find out about her. He could have kept the sight of Bathsheba as a private memory, but he didn't; he sent a servant to see if she was available. When the servant returned, with news that she was married and, therefore, unavailable, David took his third, deliberate step: he sent for her.

Finally, having sent for her, he slept with her. All along the way, there were opportunities to change course. This was no 'whirlwind' of temptation—it rarely is—and, had David been with his troops, he would never have been on that rooftop at all.

This account of David's sin is very personal, but it's about more than the man; it's about David the king. Can he act as he pleases? If he were a neighbouring king, the answer would be 'Yes', but he is the king of Israel, appointed by God and answerable to him. David should not act as he pleases; he must act as pleases God and, in this, he is no different from anyone else.

Reflection

When I'm tempted, do I have no choice or many choices?

DR

2 SAMUEL 11:5–9 (NIV)

Plan A

The woman conceived and sent word to David, saying, 'I am pregnant.' So David sent this word to Joab: 'Send me Uriah the Hittite.' And Joab sent him to David. When Uriah came to him, David asked him how Joab was, how the soldiers were and how the war was going. Then David said to Uriah, 'Go down to your house and wash your feet.' So Uriah left the palace, and a gift from the king was sent after him. But Uriah slept at the entrance to the palace with all his master's servants and did not go down to his house.

In today's reading, the millennia that separate us from David shrink to nothing. He is a man who wanted sex but not the consequences—a woman, pregnant in a culture where abortion is impossible, who hands all responsibility back to him!

David begins to scheme. Uriah is away so the child is clearly not his, but the king comes up with a plan. He brings Uriah back from the war for a little rest and relaxation. He asks him for news of the fighting, makes a fuss of him and sends him home with a present and a bit of nudge-nudge, wink-wink man-to-man slang. If Uriah does indeed 'wash his feet' (a traditional euphemism for 'have sex' in that culture) with Bathsheba, she can claim that the child is his.

Uriah has other ideas, however. He is a leader who feels that it is wrong for him to snuggle up with his wife while his men are camped out on the battlefield. Instead of going home, he bivouacs in the palace courtyard. The next morning, when David finds out, he throws a party, encourages Uriah to drink heavily and sends him home… again. Uriah, again, does not go.

There is only one way to deal with sin and it's the pattern set out in both the old and new covenants—accept what we've done, admit it, repent of it and trust ourselves to God. The human pattern for dealing with sin is very different: sin, deny, evade, justify, obfuscate or, to put it another way, sin, sin, sin, sin and sin again. We see it in David, Adam and Eve, and, to be honest, ourselves.

Prayer
Lord, I confess my sin.
Please forgive me.

DR

Plan B

In the morning David wrote a letter to Joab and sent it with Uriah. In it he wrote, 'Put Uriah in the front line where the fighting is fiercest. Then withdraw from him so that he will be struck down and die.' So while Joab had the city under siege, he put Uriah at a place where he knew the strongest defenders were. When the men of the city came out and fought against Joab, some of David's army fell; moreover, Uriah the Hittite died.

When David gives Uriah this message to take back to Joab, Uriah doesn't realize that it's his own death sentence. Let's go back over the chain of events that have led to this terrible point. David has, for reasons of his own, stopped fighting with his men. Instead, he has watched Bathsheba, found out about her, sent for her, slept with her and then, to cover up the adultery, sent Uriah to sleep with his wife (twice). Now Uriah will die and all because David, relaxing while others fought, watched Bathsheba bathe. There's an old proverb: 'For want of a nail the shoe was lost; for want of a shoe the horse was lost; for want of a horse the battle was lost; for want of a battle the kingdom was lost— and all for the want of a horseshoe nail.' When it comes to sin, there's no distinction between the nail and the kingdom, which is why Jesus teaches as he does about adultery and anger in Matthew 5:21–22, 27–28. In God's econ-omy, 'watching' is no different from 'doing', but how wise it is to ask for forgiveness at an early stage!

In this story, David's sin leads directly to Uriah's death. This should come as no surprise, though, as sin always leads to death (Romans 6:23). That's what sin does, from the Garden of Eden onwards. Sometimes sin rebounds directly on the sinner, like a deadly boomerang, but more often than not, it's others who pay the price and, in a world where everyone sins, the price is very high. God understands this, of course. When Jesus went willingly to the cross, he offered his life to pay for all (Romans 7:23), including David and us.

Prayer

Lord, forgive me when I take sin, and your death, lightly.

DR

2 SAMUEL 11:18–21, 25–27 (NIV, ABRIDGED)

Life goes on

Joab sent David a full account of the battle. He instructed the messenger... 'Say to him, "Also, your servant Uriah the Hittite is
dead."'... David told the messenger, 'Say this to Joab: "Don't let
this upset you; the sword devours one as well as another. Press the
attack against the city and destroy it." Say this to encourage Joab.'
When Uriah's wife heard that her husband was dead, she mourned
for him. After the time of mourning was over, David had her brought
to his house, and she became his wife and bore him a son. But the
thing David had done displeased the Lord.

On the face of it, life goes on. David is still king; the war continues; Bathsheba mourns Uriah, marries David and gives birth to their son. Those who know the secret keep it and David becomes philosophical, saying (more or less), 'OK, Uriah's dead, but so are lots of other men', implying, 'Maybe Uriah would have been killed anyway.'

It looks as if David has got away with it, but God knows what he's done and this is the same God who made Saul king and then removed the crown from him and his descendants. Psalm 51:11 contains a heartfelt plea: 'Do not cast me from your presence or take your Holy Spirit from me'. This is what happened to Saul; it could also happen to David.

Yesterday we thought about the way in which the consequences of our sin may be experienced most directly by others. This can lead us to think that our sin carries no consequences, but, even when life seems to go on with nothing much changing, there are, indeed, consequences to sin. We never 'get away with it' because God always knows where the fault lies. God is light so nothing remains concealed or hidden (Luke 12:2–3) and everything will be disclosed and made known.

So, do we wait for God's judgment in the future or submit to it here and now? When we admit our sin, seek forgiveness and trust Christ, we accept judgment now, but Jesus, out of his love for us, accepts the judgment for our sin (2 Corinthians 5:17–19).

Reflection and prayer

*'Who will rescue me from this body
of death? Thanks be to God—
through Jesus Christ our Lord!'*
(Romans 7:24–25)

DR

2 Samuel 12:1–4 (NIV, abridged)

Confrontation

The Lord sent Nathan to David. When he came to him, he said, 'There were two men in a certain town, one rich and the other poor. The rich man had a very large number of sheep and cattle, but the poor man had nothing except one little ewe lamb that he had bought... It was like a daughter to him. Now a traveller came to the rich man, but the rich man refrained from taking one of his own sheep or cattle to prepare a meal for the traveller... Instead, he took the ewe lamb that belonged to the poor man and prepared it for the one who had come to him.'

Seneca (4BC–AD65) said, 'Other men's sins are before our eyes; our own are behind our backs'. It's an aphorism that suits David precisely and reminds us that there are always three points of view—how we see ourselves, how other people see us and how God sees us. We may have unrealistically positive or negative views about ourselves, and so may other people, but God always sees us just as we are.

David seems to have reached a very 21st-century accommodation with his behaviour. He has 'moved on in a guilt-free expression of self-acceptance', to use contemporary jargon! In other words, his sin is 'behind his back', where he can't see it, and in front of him are all the reasons, explanations and justifications that turn 'wrong' into 'right'. David has convinced himself that all is well.

What other people thought of him is not clear, but, whatever they thought, they kept quiet. Only a very brave servant would criticize the king to his face. Nathan must have felt that he'd drawn a very short straw when God sent him to challenge David, but God's method of challenge is not ours. We tend to go for face-to-face accusations; God prefers to reach 'behind our backs' and place before us what has been out of our sight and, to do this, he inspires Nathan's parable.

When Jesus spoke in parables, it was no new thing. God has always used parables—and he still does—because they sidestep our opinion of ourselves, make the opinions of others irrelevant and allow us to look directly at the truth, which is what God sees.

Prayer

Lord, teach me to see as you see.

DR

2 SAMUEL 12:5–10, 13 (NIV, ABRIDGED)

Judgment

David burned with anger against the man and said to Nathan, 'As surely as the Lord lives, the man who did this deserves to die!...' Then Nathan said to David, 'You are the man! This is what the Lord, the God of Israel, says: "I anointed you king over Israel, and I delivered you from the hand of Saul... Why did you despise the word of the Lord by doing what is evil in his eyes? You struck down Uriah the Hittite with the sword and took his wife to be your own. You killed him with the sword of the Ammonites. Now, therefore, the sword shall never depart from your house, because you despised me..." Then David said to Nathan, 'I have sinned against the Lord.'

David is incensed by Nathan's parable and he quickly judges and condemns the 'rich man'. He is condemning himself, of course, and when Nathan points this out, David's view of himself changes. His self-justification evaporates and he is left looking at what was 'behind his back'—the truth of his sin. He responds in a way that shows his basic integrity; he owns up.

If we are tempted to dismiss the Old Testament as too gory, too ancient or too culturally different or concerned with a different religion, it's good to read passages such as this. Here we see God cutting across history, through culture and religion. That afternoon, David experienced the presence of God and was humbled. His reaction was the same as Simon's on the day when Jesus took him fishing (Luke 5:4–8) and the same as that of every other person who has experienced the presence of God, because we never experience God without experiencing ourselves and we then realize how far short of God's intentions we have fallen.

We can arrive at knowledge of our sin through honest reflection; conviction of sin, though, is a work of the Spirit of God (John 16:7–11). David lived under the old covenant whereas we live under the new covenant, but God has not changed. Self-knowledge tends to lead to accommodation, but conviction leads to change and that is God's desire, for those who lived in ancient palaces and us in our modern homes.

Reflection

'The word of God is living and active... it judges the thoughts and attitudes of the heart'
(Hebrews 4:12).

DR

2 Samuel 12:15–18, 20, 24 (NIV, abridged)

The verdict

After Nathan had gone home, the Lord struck the child that Uriah's wife had borne to David, and he became ill. David pleaded with God for the child. He fasted and went into his house and spent the nights lying on the ground. The elders of his household stood beside him to get him up from the ground, but he refused, and he would not eat any food with them. On the seventh day the child died... Then David got up from the ground. After he had washed, put on lotions and changed his clothes, he went into the house of the Lord and worshipped... Then David comforted his wife Bathsheba, and he went to her and lay with her. She gave birth to a son, and they named him Solomon.

As modern-day readers, our first question is, 'Did God really strike the child and make him ill?' However we choose to answer that question, one thing is clear: David evidently thought the answer was 'Yes' and so did the writer of 2 Samuel. Given that this was David's viewpoint, it's fruitful to consider his response. He didn't shout or blame—he pleaded and fasted. As far as David was concerned, he was to blame and God was within his rights to remove him as king and bring his lineage to an abrupt halt.

David wastes no time longing for what could have been. He accepts what is and concurs with what he considers to be God's judgment. His hope is that God will relent and allow the child to live and he makes it as clear as he can to God that he understands that the sin is his, not the child's. When the baby dies, though, David cleans himself up and then goes to worship, to get 'cleaned up' on the inside.

David's behaviour may seem strange to us (v. 21 shows that it seemed pretty strange to his own servants, too), but David is making sense of his encounter with God. As far as he is concerned, his own sin has led to the death of the child. The old covenant is clear: sin always leads to death. God's truth in the new covenant is still ahead, when the death of one covers the sins of all.

Prayer

Thank you, Lord, that in your death I find life.

DR

2 Samuel 13:1–2, 6, 11–14 (NIV, abridged)

Desire

Amnon son of David fell in love with Tamar, the beautiful sister of Absalom son of David. Amnon became frustrated to the point of illness on account of his sister Tamar, for she was a virgin, and it seemed impossible for him to do anything to her… So Amnon lay down and pretended to be ill. When the king came to see him, Amnon said to him, 'I would like my sister Tamar to come and make some special bread in my sight, so that I may eat from her hand.'… But when she took it to him to eat, he grabbed her and said, 'Come to bed with me, my sister.' 'Don't, my brother!' she said to him. '… Don't do this wicked thing…' But he refused to listen to her, and since he was stronger than she, he raped her.

To us, the central issue here is incest, but, in ancient cultures, royal households often allowed sibling marriages and, in some countries, such marriages were obligatory (the Pharaohs in Egypt, for example). Amnon and Tamar had different mothers and, as she points out to him, if he really wants her, he can ask the king for permission to marry her (see v. 13). It's not his desire that devastates Tamar or even the thought of sex with him—it's being forced into sex outside marriage.

Amnon is consumed with lust so his sexual frustration permeates his every waking moment. On the advice of a friend, he hatches this plot to get Tamar alone and then, regardless of the consequences, he forces himself on her. It's at this moment that phrases such as 'like father like son' have a terrible resonance. In his own way, Amnon has behaved with Tamar in a similar fashion to David with Bathsheba, so everything that was said about David's temptation applies here as well. Amnon could have turned from his lust, but, instead, he nursed it and took steps to turn temptation into reality.

There's a rule of creation here that applies from Genesis onwards: godly desire leads to satisfaction, but sinful desire leads to sin, more sin and yet more sin. Amnon was tempted into thinking that he could have consequence-free sex—he was deceiving himself.

Reflection

'An evil man is snared by his own sin, but a righteous one can sing and be glad' (Proverbs 29:6).

DR

Hatred

Then Amnon hated her with intense hatred. In fact, he hated her more than he had loved her... And Tamar lived in her brother Absalom's house, a desolate woman. When King David heard all this, he was furious. Absalom never said a word to Amnon, either good or bad; he hated Amnon because he had disgraced his sister Tamar. Two years later... Absalom ordered his men, 'Listen! When Amnon is in high spirits from drinking wine and I say to you, "Strike Amnon down," then kill him. Don't be afraid. Have not I given you this order? Be strong and brave.' So Absalom's men did to Amnon what Absalom had ordered.

Absalom takes Tamar under his wing and is outwardly polite to Amnon, but inside he nurses his hatred until he engineers an opportunity to kill him. Absalom then exiles himself, leaving David to grieve for both of these sons—one dead and another lost (vv. 34–38).

As these plots and events take place around him, David seems to be helpless. He's like the blindfolded adult in a game of blind man's buff where the children run around him, just out of reach. This is no game, though, and the deadly consequences of past sinful actions continue in all too real a fashion. Most of us can sympathize with David—we haven't (I hope) experienced our children plotting each other's deaths, but there have probably been times when events have unfolded around us and we've felt powerless to change them. All we could do was to watch and grieve.

In David's case, the seeds of these events were deliberate sins and, while that is not always the cause, it's worth stepping back from a situation and asking God, 'Am I, in any way, the cause of this?'

It's sad to see David, the golden boy, revealed as such a tarnished man, but it's notable that, in spite of what was happening, he continued to love his sons. If we are tempted to ask, 'Why doesn't God do something? Why doesn't he intervene?' the answer is this: 'Because God is love'. Just as the end of the chapter shows David waiting for Absalom's return, regardless of what he's done, so God waits for David... and us.

Reflection

'Above all, love each other deeply, because love covers over a multitude of sins' (1 Peter 4:8).

DR

2 SAMUEL 14:1–3, 5–8 (NIV, ABRIDGED)

Reconciliation

Joab son of Zeruiah knew that the king's heart longed for Absalom. So Joab sent someone to Tekoa and had a wise woman brought from there. He said to her, 'Pretend you are in mourning... Then go to the king and speak these words to him'... The king asked her, 'What is troubling you?' She said '... I your servant had two sons. They got into a fight with each other in the field, and no one was there to separate them. One struck the other and killed him. Now the whole clan has risen up against your servant; they say, "Hand over the one who struck his brother down, so that we may put him to death for the life of his brother whom he killed."'... The king said to the woman, 'Go home, and I will issue an order on your behalf.'

Joab responds to David's continued distress by taking action. We are not told whether he remembered Nathan's parable or not, but the same approach works again. David listens to the woman's story and orders that the wayward son should return home unmolested, at which point she reveals that her story is really about Absalom (see vv. 13–21). David is persuaded and invites his son home, but not back to the palace and not to his court for two years (vv. 23–24).

Why David behaved in this way is unclear; what is clear is that Absalom took his opportunities with both hands and multiplied them. For four years, he made himself available to everyone who sought judgment from David, sympathized with them and wistfully mentioned that, if he was in charge, everything would be so different! In this way, he built a powerbase of popularity, as chapter 15 tells.

What did David do about this threat to his kingship? Seemingly, nothing. It's possible that he didn't know what was going on or that he knew but felt helpless. It's possible that he loved Absalom so much that he refused to confront him. It may also be, as Jesus says, that 'the people of this world are more shrewd in dealing with their own kind than are the people of the light' (Luke 16:8). Maybe David's inaction wasn't a sign of weakness but of the godly naivety that we call righteousness.

Reflection

How much do our judgments of others reveal about ourselves?

DR

2 SAMUEL 15:13–14, 25–26 (NIV)

Rebellion

A messenger came and told David, 'The hearts of the men of Israel are with Absalom.' Then David said to all his officials who were with him in Jerusalem, 'Come! We must flee, or none of us will escape from Absalom. We must leave immediately, or he will move quickly to overtake us and bring ruin upon us and put the city to the sword.'... Then the king said to Zadok [the priest], 'Take the ark of God back into the city. If I find favour in the Lord's eyes, he will bring me back and let me see it and his dwelling place again. But if he says, "I am not pleased with you," then I am ready; let him do to me whatever seems good to him.'

As Absalom grabs for power, David goes on the run—again! He spent years avoiding Saul (1 Samuel 19—30) and he must have thought that those days were far behind him. Now that he faces exile for the second time, his reaction to this disaster is mixed. He exhibits a fine sense of political cunning by leaving behind in Jerusalem certain allies who will spy on his son for him and keep him abreast of Absalom's plans. At the same time, he trusts God with his future, saying that, whether he returns to Jerusalem or meets his death, he is ready for God's will and purpose. In a way, this sums David up: he was a man who had many faults and weaknesses, but he lived his life with an unwavering faith in God.

That where we have to leave these readings—with David facing up to the consequences of his past (his disobedience to God; his sins, poor judgments and terrible family life) and looking ahead to more betrayal and bereavement. In many ways, he was a worse king than Saul, so the question is, 'Why did God oust Saul and stick with David?' The answer is simple: Saul never repented, but David always did. Serving God has never been about getting everything right, but about trusting ourselves to God's love and forgiveness.

Prayer

'Search me, O God, and know my heart; test me and know my anxious thoughts. See if there is any offensive way in me, and lead me in the way everlasting'
(Psalm 139:23–24).

DR

1 Corinthians 14—16

Welcome back to Paul the fire-fighter—or, maybe, Paul the trouble-shooter. The church in Corinth was on fire for God, but it was also plagued with outrageous moral behaviour, worship services full of chaos and confusion, people with basic misunderstandings of the gospel. Perhaps some of that is all too familiar!

In our readings, Paul begins by offering guidance for their worship. There was a great cacophony of speaking in tongues—people were so thrilled by the spiritual gift given by God that they were using it inappropriately in worship. Now I have experienced a similar problem in a church, but, I have to confess, my more frequent experience as I visit churches is such planning and control that the greatest danger of chaos comes from the toddlers, not an over-exuberant use of charismatic gifts!

As we will see, Paul emphasizes two core principles that should still apply today: everything we do in church must be done for the benefit of the Church, our fellow members, and true worship will reflect God's character—the one who creatively brings order in place of chaos, harmony in place of discord. Then, Paul switches from the practicalities of worship to the bedrock of faith that some were doubting—the resurrection of Jesus. There is, of course, a link. Paul argues that, if there is no resurrection, there is no reality in our faith and, therefore, no basis for worship. The resurrection of Jesus is true and it is foundational to our faith. What's more, it is the sign and guarantee that those who follow Jesus in life will follow him through death into newness of life.

Faced with outrageous behaviour, chaotic worship and doctrinal wobbles, it's interesting just how much Paul speaks of love. Our readings start with the words 'Follow the way of love' and end with 'Do everything in love'. Now, as then, there is no other way to function as an individual in a church or as an individual and a church in the local and global community. It's love that enables us to cope with the worship we don't like, the people with whom we disagree. God pours his love into us—if only more Christians lived it and shared it with the same generosity. My prayer is that, as you read the apostle's words over the next two weeks, you will be encouraged to 'follow the way of love'.

Stephen Rand

1 Corinthians 14:1–5 (TNIV)

Loving prophecy

Follow the way of love and eagerly desire spiritual gifts, especially the gift of prophecy. For those who speak in a tongue do not speak to other people but to God. Indeed, no one understands them; they utter mysteries by the Spirit. But those who prophesy speak to people for their strengthening, encouragement and comfort. Those who speak in a tongue edify themselves, but those who prophesy edify the church. I would like every one of you to speak in tongues, but even more to prophesy. Those who prophesy are greater than those who speak in tongues, unless they interpret, so that the church may be edified.

These words follow perhaps the best-known chapter in the Bible: 1 Corinthians 13—Paul's inspiring description of love. In fact, though, in terms of argument, chapter 14 follows on almost directly from the end of chapter 12: 'eagerly desire the greater gifts' (12:31). It is as if Paul, grappling with the challenge of giving practical advice to those intoxicated by the excitement of spiritual gifts, remembered that the principle was simple: 'Follow the way of love' (v. 1). Simple, but so important that he felt it worth inserting the wonderful description of the way of love that is chapter 13.

It is because of his love for people that Paul commends prophecy over tongues in his discussion of spiritual gifts. Prophecy is a word from God, given through a human being, that brings 'strengthening, encouragement and comfort' (14:3). Which of us can continue in our journey with God without this kind of loving support?

Note that Paul is not against speaking in tongues—he would like everyone to have that gift—but he is emphasizing that, while the gift of tongues is great for the individual, prophecy is great for the Church. 'Edify' is the translation of a Greek word used in the building trade and Paul loved to use it to describe the real 'building up' of the Church, which is its people. Eugene Peterson in THE MESSAGE puts it like this: 'Proclaiming God's truth to the church in its common language brings the whole church into growth and strength.' That is truly a spiritual gift—and an expression of the way of love.

Reflection

God's gifts are given so others can be blessed.

SR

1 Corinthians 14:6, 9–12 (TNIV)

That makes sense

Now, brothers and sisters, if I come to you and speak in tongues, what good will I be to you, unless I bring you some revelation or knowledge or prophecy or word of instruction?... So it is with you. Unless you speak intelligible words with your tongue, how will anyone know what you are saying? You will just be speaking into the air. Undoubtedly there are all sorts of languages in the world, yet none of them is without meaning. If then I do not grasp the meaning of what someone is saying, I am a foreigner to the speaker, and the speaker is a foreigner to me. So it is with you. Since you are eager for gifts of the Spirit, try to excel in those that build up the church.

Paul believed in the power of words. He was a communicator—he loved preaching and he loved writing: just think of all his letters that we have in the New Testament. I too love preaching and writing. I think words are great—what a long speech it was at my daughter's wedding!

So, I need to take notice of Paul's instruction here. What matters is that words come from God and they are 'intelligible': they must make sense to the person who hears them. It is this combination that will build up the Church—otherwise, the words will be so much hot air (see v. 9). Paul insists that he will only be of use to them if he brings 'revelation or knowledge or prophecy or word of instruction' (v. 6). Whenever I preach I do all I can to do it well, then I pray that God will speak to those who listen, whether because of my preparation or in spite of it.

A natural gift of communication has to become a spiritual gift if it is to do people good. It doesn't mean that I have to use a strange voice or use old-fashioned words. It means that I have to seek God for his Spirit to breathe out his words through me and, if God is at work, those words will be intelligible because God wants his people to hear, to understand and respond.

Prayer

Lord, grant every one of us the gift of your Spirit, so that our words will always build up and not tear down. Amen

SR

Put your mind to it

For this reason those who speak in a tongue should pray that they may interpret what they say. For if I pray in a tongue, my spirit prays, but my mind is unfruitful. So what shall I do? I will pray with my spirit, but I will also pray with my understanding… Otherwise when you are praising God in the Spirit, how can the others, who are now put in the same situation as an enquirer, say 'Amen' to your thanksgiving, since they do not know what you are saying? You are giving thanks well enough, but the others are not edified. I thank God that I speak in tongues more than all of you. But in the church I would rather speak five intelligible words to instruct others than ten thousand words in a tongue.

You can only ride a bike when you have learned balance. Churches progress on the same basis: there needs to be a positive balance between mind and Spirit. The church in Corinth was wild with spiritual excitement, so Paul emphasizes the need to engage the brain. He was not in favour of mindless worship, but, equally, we can become so cerebral that the Holy Spirit is rationalized away and his gifts denied.

The balance needed is not a lowest common denominator of caution and fear but a positive embracing of the reality of God's supernatural power exercised with wisdom and thought. Paul wanted to pray and sing with his spirit and use his mind so that he prayed and sang with understanding. This was not only good for him. Once again, he insists that the principle is that we do what is best for others. He wants a prayer to provoke an 'Amen' because others have understood it and can agree with it. He wants to speak intelligibly in church so that others are instructed.

More and more Christians choose a church that suits them, where they 'feel at home'. Paul wanted all churches to be places where a full range of spiritual gifts is used thoughtfully for the benefit of all. I think that I could feel at home in a church like that.

Reflection

'Love the Lord your God with all your heart, soul, strength, and mind' (Luke 10:27, CEV) or, as The Message *puts it, 'with all your passion and prayer and muscle and intelligence'.*

SR

Outside looking in

So if the whole church comes together and everyone speaks in tongues, and enquirers or unbelievers come in, will they not say that you are out of your mind? But if an unbeliever or an enquirer comes in while everyone is prophesying, they are convicted of sin and are brought under judgment by all, as the secrets of their hearts are laid bare. So they will fall down and worship God, exclaiming, 'God is really among you!'

Songs of Praise reminds me that worship is not a spectator sport. As soon as people stop thinking about singing and start focusing on God, they look as if they are visiting another planet—which, in one sense, they are.

Paul has argued that prophecy is better than tongues in building up the church. Now he considers their impact on 'outsiders'. Intelligibility is still key. Visitors hearing a multitude of unknown languages may conclude that Christians are raving, but, if they hear clear words of prophecy revealing that God, through his people, knows all about them, their reaction will be very different: they will be called to repentance and worship. Once again, Paul reveals his concern for people, especially those outside the church family. He wants them to hear and understand the words of eternal life.

These verses are strikingly relevant. How can our services allow Christians to worship with freedom and depth and hear teaching that brings insight, challenge and encouragement, without making them too long, too strange or too demanding for those on the edge of the church? One answer has been 'seeker services', primarily designed for those as yet uncommitted but willing to be there on a Sunday.

I simply offer three principles, which are consistent with Paul's concerns. First, the church exists for mission: it must be more concerned about reaching the 'outsider' than the comfort of its own members. Second, worship must be real, in spirit and truth (John 4:24): visitors always see through pretence. Third, churches must face the challenge of growing disciples: one hour of Sunday worship is rarely enough to develop understanding, enthusiasm and commitment.

Reflection

How likely is it that a visitor to your church would react by saying, 'God is really among you'?

SR

The harmony of creative worship

When you come together, each of you has a hymn, or a word of instruction, a revelation, a tongue or an interpretation. Everything must be done so that the church may be built up. If anyone speaks in a tongue, two—or at the most three—should speak, one at a time, and someone must interpret. If there is no interpreter, the speaker should keep quiet in the church; let them speak to themselves and to God. Two or three prophets should speak, and the others should weigh carefully what is said... For you can all prophesy in turn so that everyone may be instructed and encouraged... For God is not a God of disorder but of peace.

In Corinth, there was no pre-planned order of service, directed by a 'professional' at the front. Instead, everyone came with something to contribute: worship was a participatory experience. Paul endorses this, but adds: just make sure that each contribution is for building up the whole church, not for showing off or self-fulfilment.

Speaking in a tongue is fine, he says, but it must be one person at a time, with an interpretation given so that everyone can benefit from it. Paul is clear: there is a gift of speaking in tongues that enables the speaker to express worship when words are inadequate, and this is for private use. There is also a supernatural gift of speaking in a tongue capable of being interpreted. When this gift is used in worship, it can—and should—build up the church. Prophecy is the same: one person at a time should speak, taking care that the words are weighed, so that the church can benefit.

These charismatic gifts are not so supernatural that they are beyond human control. Those so gifted can choose to be silent. Paul writes because, in Corinth, that was not done often enough. In my experience, most churches today have the opposite problem: there is little or no space for these gifts to be exercised.

God does not give gifts to create chaos or confusion. He is a God of peace—or, in this context, perhaps 'harmony' is a better word. We know that God's Spirit is inspiring worship when a multitude of contributions join to create an ordered, life-giving and life-filled whole.

Prayer

Lord, may we know your order and your peace as we worship together.

SR

1 CORINTHIANS 14:34–35 (TNIV)

Women and worship

Women should remain silent in the churches. They are not allowed to speak, but must be in submission, as the law says. If they want to enquire about something, they should ask their own husbands at home; for it is disgraceful for a woman to speak in the church.

How much debate, frustration, pain and broken fellowship have resulted from these two short verses? How much God-given wisdom has been lost to the Church because women have been forced to remain silent? How many women have given up on God because men used these verses to enforce what they sincerely believed to be a biblical stance? The instruction certainly appears straightforward and is very strongly worded, but, a few chapters earlier, Paul tells women how they should pray and prophesy in church (11:5–6), so, clearly, at that point he was not expecting them to be silent.

In the New Testament, women are given a radical new status. Jesus scandalized traditionalists by giving them equal opportunities to hear from him and minister to him. Paul indicates that, in the Church, gender barriers are broken down and, within marriage, submission is to be mutual, giving an equality of rights. Women are fellow missionaries with Paul, in church leadership, praying and prophesying.

So, how do we make sense of the instruction above? The word 'speak' is the word used for people addressing the whole congregation, so these verses are not simply telling women to avoid chatter during services. It is just possible that Paul did not write these verses— that they were a later addition.

My suggestion is that, while no one is sure which law Paul is referring to here, the use of the word 'submission'—which Paul insists elsewhere is a mutual submission of men and women to one another —hints that, in Corinth, there was a specific problem with women speaking out of turn, perhaps interrupting worship to ask inappropriate questions. If this is the case, then the general principle being put forward here is not that women are to be silent partners in worship, but, rather, that 'everything should be done in a fitting and orderly way' (14:40).

Prayer

Lord, grant us your wisdom to know when we need to be silent and the times when we need to speak up.

SR

The gospel

For what I received I passed on to you as of first importance: that Christ died for our sins according to the scriptures, that he was buried, that he was raised on the third day according to the scriptures, and that he appeared to Cephas, and then to the Twelve. After that, he appeared to more than five hundred of the brothers and sisters at the same time, most of whom are still living, though some have fallen asleep. Then he appeared to James, then to all the apostles, and last of all he appeared to me also, as to one abnormally born.

Paul closes his letter by turning from the practices of the church in worship to its beliefs and, in fact, the most important doctrine of all: the resurrection of Jesus Christ. There were clearly some in the church at Corinth who held the view that there was no such thing as the resurrection of the dead— not an uncommon view in our own society, even within the Church. Paul therefore launches into a lengthy defence of his insistence that Jesus is alive.

To Paul this is absolutely crucial. It is the 'good news' of the gospel and 'By this gospel you are saved' (v. 2). This is foundational to the Corinthians' faith and, therefore, their worship—take it away and the basis of Christianity is removed.

This is exactly my experience. When I left home and became a history student, I had to decide whether the faith that I had learned from my parents was going to become my own or not. I would have been quite glad to shake it off, but I couldn't rid myself of the conviction that Jesus really did rise from the dead and, if that was true, everything else had to be true.

Paul starts by simply stating the facts. Jesus died, was buried and then he was seen, alive. He offers these facts for verification. At that time, most of the people who had seen Jesus alive after he had died were still around. There's an unspoken challenge here: if you don't believe it, go and cross-examine the witnesses. Two thousand years later, the eyewitnesses have gone, of course, but their witness remains, so the challenge is the same: check the facts.

Reflection
Thank God that our faith is not a leap in the dark, but rooted in historical fact. Jesus is alive!

SR

1 CORINTHIANS 15:12–14, 17–19 (TNIV)

Hope, not futility

But if it is preached that Christ has been raised from the dead, how can some of you say that there is no resurrection of the dead? If there is no resurrection of the dead, then not even Christ has been raised. And if Christ has not been raised, our preaching is useless and so is your faith... And if Christ has not been raised, your faith is futile; you are still in your sins. Then those also who have fallen asleep in Christ are lost. If only for this life we have hope in Christ, we are to be pitied more than all others.

For Paul it was simple logic. If there was no such thing as resurrection, then Jesus could not have been raised from the dead and, if Jesus had not been not raised from the dead, then faith was futile. This is because, to Paul, faith was knowing Jesus died so sins could be forgiven and we could be restored to a relationship with God that would not, and could not, be broken by death.

It's possible that there were those in Corinth who believed in life after death, but as a survival of the spirit rather than the resurrection of the body. Thus, Paul first emphasized (in yesterday's reading) that Jesus was seen—because he had a body there was something to see! That is what he had preached. If their faith was based on his preaching and they didn't believe that part of it, what basis had they for believing the rest? They were implying that Paul had lied about God.

Now, many people today believe in the survival of the spirit rather than the resurrection of the body—many probably worshipping in church today—so why does Paul insist that the resurrection of the body is essential to the Christian faith? The answer lies in his understanding of what God did when Jesus died and rose again. God was restoring his creation, rebuilding all that had been broken by sin. There was to be a new heaven and a new earth. Life after death was not a continuation of this life. It was—and is—a new life to be lived: body, mind and spirit all made new.

Prayer

Father, as your Church worships you today, grant a fresh vision of the risen Christ.

SR

1 CORINTHIANS 15:20–26 (TNIV)

The last enemy

But Christ has indeed been raised from the dead, the firstfruits of those who have fallen asleep. For since death came through a human being, the resurrection of the dead comes also through a human being. For as in Adam all die, so in Christ all will be made alive. But in this order: Christ, the firstfruits; then, when he comes, those who belong to him. Then the end will come, when he hands over the kingdom to God the Father after he has destroyed all dominion, authority and power. For he must reign until he has put all his enemies under his feet. The last enemy to be destroyed is death.

I can't read these words without hearing in my mind the glorious music of Handel's *Messiah*. Somehow, the composer captures the triumph of the contrast between death and life that also exists in these words. The solemn, funereal notes of the music remind us that, because we are all children of Adam, we share in the death that resulted from his sin. The explosion of energy in the notes that follow exemplifies the life that comes from being born again as the children of God.

'The wages of sin is death' (Romans 6:23). In Paul's understanding of the gospel, sin had broken all human relationships— with God, with each other, with the environment. In God's presence, Adam and Eve experienced life; sent out from Paradise they had to face the reality of death.

Death was the ultimate sign and reality of the damage done by sin. Thus, the ultimate sign and reality of God destroying the impact of sin was the destruction of death itself. The sign that death has been destroyed is the resurrection of the body to eternal life.

These verses resonate with the glorious vision of what God has done in and through Jesus. His resurrection is a sign and a promise of the resurrection in which his people will share. He will triumph, he will reign. He is truly victorious. That's why Christians can say that, while they may fear dying, they do not fear death.

Prayer

Holy God, Loving Father, thank you for the completeness of the victory of Jesus and the promise of eternal life. Begin your reign in me, so that I may know your life and share in your victory. Amen

SR

1 Corinthians 15:35–38, 42–44 (TNIV)

A spiritual body

But someone will ask, 'How are the dead raised? With what kind of body will they come?' How foolish! What you sow does not come to life unless it dies. When you sow, you do not plant the body that will be, but just a seed, perhaps of wheat or of something else. But God gives it a body as he has determined, and to each kind of seed he gives its own body... So will it be with the resurrection of the dead. The body that is sown is perishable, it is raised imperishable; it is sown in dishonour, it is raised in glory; it is sown in weakness, it is raised in power; it is sown a natural body, it is raised a spiritual body.

Two questions: Paul answers the second one first (we'll read his answer to the first tomorrow). Those who doubted the possibility of a physical resurrection were asking what a resurrection body would be like—a question Paul regards as foolish. Why? Because behind the question was the assumption that if you couldn't imagine the resurrection body, you couldn't imagine the resurrection and Paul saw this as a failure to acknowledge the power of God.

So, he embarks on a sermon from science, using basic biology to illustrate the way God works: a seed is planted, it dies and comes to life as something different but related. Each seed brings forth its own specific kind of body: animals are different from birds, birds are different from fish (v. 39).

The key point is that God determines this process—the body that results from the seed is decided by God's creative choices. He is more than capable of producing and providing what Paul calls a 'spiritual body', one designed by God and therefore perfectly 'fit for purpose'.

Many in Corinth would have been shocked by the idea of a spiritual body. The common cultural belief was that spirit and body were distinct and incompatible. Paul gives a very different picture, with a series of vivid contrasts. The body we know now is subject to decay, weakness and death; the resurrection body will be gloriously full of strength and life, designed for living with God in the new creation. Brilliant!

Prayer

Lord, grant your strength to those struggling with their physical body. Fill them with your hope for their future.

SR

1 CORINTHIANS 15:50–53, 56–57 (TNIV)

We will be changed

I declare to you, brothers and sisters, that flesh and blood cannot inherit the kingdom of God, nor does the perishable inherit the imperishable. Listen, I tell you a mystery: we will not all sleep, but we will all be changed—in a flash, in the twinkling of an eye, at the last trumpet. For the trumpet will sound, the dead will be raised imperishable, and we will be changed. For the perishable must clothe itself with the imperishable, and the mortal with immortality... The sting of death is sin, and the power of sin is the law. But thanks be to God! He gives us the victory through our Lord Jesus Christ.

Paul returns to the first question he raised in verse 35: 'How are the dead raised?' The answer is clearer after his explanation of the 'spiritual body'. If the difference between what we are now and what we will be is so great, there is a gap to be bridged. If 'flesh and blood cannot inherit the kingdom of God' (v. 50), then God will have to act: 'we will all be changed' (v. 51).

Both those who have died and those still alive will need the new body for life in the new kingdom, but that is no problem for God. He is in the business of transformation and, just as he breathed life into the first human being in a moment, in a flash the transformation will take place.

'The trumpet will sound' (v. 52). The jubilee trumpet was to sound on the great day of forgiveness as a sign of God's decisive intervention in human history (Leviticus 25:9). In the synagogue at Nazareth, Jesus announced that Isaiah's reference to the jubilee was fulfilled in him (Luke 4:18–21): the echo of the trumpet was heard again. One day, says Paul, the trumpet will sound and God's work in Jesus will be complete.

It's not automatic, 'our natural, earthy lives don't in themselves lead us by their very nature into the kingdom of God. Their very "how" is to die, so how could they "naturally" end up in the Life kingdom?' (v. 50, THE MESSAGE), but God's offer of transformation for life in his kingdom is open to all who will trust him. The promise of victory is for everyone who commits their life to Christ.

Prayer
Great God, thank you for your transforming power.

SR

1 CORINTHIANS 15:58 (TNIV)

Your labour is not in vain

Therefore, my dear brothers and sisters, stand firm. Let nothing move you. Always give yourselves fully to the work of the Lord, because you know that your labour in the Lord is not in vain.

Paul has described the promise of victory, the fulfilment of God's great project of personal and community transformation and renewal. Suddenly he feels a great tenderness for the church in Corinth that had caused him such grief by their excess and thoughtless behaviour. He wants them to live in the light of the transformation that is to come. He wants them to take all the inspiration and comfort they can from the triumph that is assured.

He has two specific exhortations for them that flow out of the assertion of God's victory. The first is to 'stand firm'. I'm old enough to remember singing a chorus in my Crusader class that went, 'Be steadfast, unmovable; by faith stand your ground.' To my youthful imagination, it always sounded so heroic—like the soldier who refused to give way even as the battle turned against him.

It's a helpful picture, except that the battle we face, as the Corinthian Christians did, is not so much a physical assault as the battle to hold on to our faith against the flow of contemporary culture and the sometimes bitter reality of personal experience. These realities may undermine the security of our faith and convince us that our involvement in serving God in the Church or in the community is not worth the effort. Paul wants us to lift our eyes, see the flag flying in victory over the battlefield and give ourselves over once again to the task.

I had a friend who was serving God in Ethiopia when he was killed in an air crash. His funeral was moving as, one after another, people told how his life had made a difference to theirs. Then, a contemporary of his, a church minister, stood up and thanked the ladies who had taught them both in Sunday school. Their faithfulness had born fruit in the lives of their young pupils. His message echoes Paul's: whatever service you give God, it does matter, it does count, it is worth it and it is not in vain.

Prayer
Father, thank you for the privilege of serving you and the encouragement of knowing that no effort we expend for you is wasted.

SR

The collection

Now about the collection for the Lord's people: do what I told the Galatian churches to do. On the first day of every week, each one of you should set aside a sum of money in keeping with your income, saving it up, so that when I come no collections will have to be made. Then, when I arrive, I will give letters of introduction to the men you approve and send them with your gift to Jerusalem. If it seems advisable for me to go also, they will accompany me.

Paul is coming to the end of his letter, but an important question needs to be answered. They had asked about Paul's relief fund collection—the church in Jerusalem was in the middle of a famine—and he turns from the great victory of Christ to the matter of taking care of God's people.

To the apostle this was not a lesser matter. Christ's death and resurrection created a new family, which must live in the light of his victory. Just as God had given to them, so they should give to others. 'Since you excel in everything… see that you also excel in this grace of giving,' Paul wrote in his next letter (2 Corinthians 8:7).

In one sentence, he outlines a simple pattern for Christian giving, as relevant today as it was then. Giving should not be an afterthought or an occasional emotional response, but regular (on the first day of every week), shared by all (each one of you), planned and systematic (set aside a sum of money)

and proportional (in keeping with your income).

We need to be organized as well as generous in our giving—spontaneous giving will usually be less generous than organized giving! We can also organize for spontaneity—regularly putting money aside so that we can respond when a need arises, trying to be sure that being organized doesn't prevent us from being softhearted and open-handed.

Churches, too, should follow Paul's guidance, regularly, systematically and proportionately ensuring that the wider church family is blessed as we have been blessed. I will confess to resenting preachers who apply Paul's words about helping the poor to giving to their church funds! Proper support of our churches is vital, but they should be models of generosity.

Prayer

God of compassion, give us the grace to give generously of all that we have.

SR

1 CORINTHIANS 16:13–14 (TNIV)

The last word

> Be on your guard; stand firm in the faith; be courageous; be strong.
> Do everything in love.

It's been a long letter; there's just time for a last set of instructions before the final greetings and personal messages.

'Be on your guard.' The original Greek word used here suggests a sentry, always alert, never relaxing. It reinforces the biblical image of life as a spiritual battle, with an enemy looking for ways to undermine and sabotage the Christian. I've seen friends lose the battle, caught unawares by personal tragedy or intellectual challenge. Professional soldiers are prepared, ready for every possibility; that's why discipleship training is so vital.

'Stand firm in the faith.' Watch any film of a Roman army in battle and you will realize that once someone stumbled or fell they were lost. That's why they fought standing close together, mutually supporting each other, making it harder to fall. A properly functioning church will be a place of mutual support, the people helping each other to stand firm in the faith.

'Be courageous; be strong.' It has been a sobering privilege recently to meet Christians facing life-threatening persecution—a young woman praying for those who have threatened to crucify her; a man risking death to share the gospel. Your situation may require a different kind of courage and strength—to tell a friend that you are a Christian or to cope with pain on a daily basis—but God's promise is that he will give you the strength you need.

'Do everything in love.' There's nothing military about this instruction, but, be assured, it is a call to use the greatest weapon in the battle. In the church, do everything in love. At home, at work, at play, do everything in love. Think of others; think how you would like to be treated in that position and then treat others like that. The only way we can begin to approach the possibility of doing everything in love is if we are on guard, standing firm in our faith, full of the courage and strength that come from God himself.

Prayer

Lord, help me to keep my eyes open, hold tight to my convictions, give it all I've got, be resolute, and love without stopping. Amen
(Based on 1 Corinthians 16:13–14,
THE MESSAGE)

SR

Mary Magdalene and the Gospel women

'Mary Magdalene—she was married to Jesus, wasn't she?' I overheard this conversation between two workmen in a local café a while ago, just when the film of the controversial (and bestselling) book *The Da Vinci Code* had come out.

Legends and rumours about Mary have always abounded and this 'Jesus' wife' story is one of the oldest, along with a theory that there still exists a secret group of people descended from their union. Another, also very old, story about Mary is that she was a prostitute, and artists have delighted in portraying her repentant at Jesus' feet, wiping them with her long and abundant hair.

In fact, the Gospels have precisely zero evidence for either of these traditions. Mary, from the town of Magdala on the western shore of Lake Galilee, was certainly an important disciple of Jesus and is named as present at key events, notably the crucifixion and the resurrection of Jesus. The name 'Mary', however, was one of the commonest of the time and several other Marys are named as associated with Jesus: his mother Mary, of course, Martha's sister Mary of Bethany and the mysterious 'Mary the mother of Joses'. It is misleading to identify Mary of Magdala with any of these other women or with unnamed women of the Gospels with whom she is also often confused.

When we disentangle, as far as possible, these various Marys and other Gospel women, we find that there is a large circle of women following Jesus, from the time when his ministry began in Galilee. The way Jesus related to these named and unnamed women is extraordinary for his time and they have much to teach us about both following him and the standing of women among his followers.

For this reason, and because there is little material specifically about Mary Magdalene, I have chosen readings that focus on other women Jesus encountered as well as on Mary, who was possibly his closest female follower. She, and they, show us that, in the kingdom Jesus came to proclaim, women are by no means secondary—in fact, they play a key role in receiving and announcing the good news. They stand for, and give hope to, all women who are abused, oppressed or suffering in body or mind. I believe they offer themselves as role models to men, too.

Veronica Zundel

Resourceful women

[Jesus] went on through cities and villages, proclaiming and bringing the good news of the kingdom of God. The twelve were with him, as well as some women who had been cured of evil spirits and infirmities: Mary, called Magdalene, from whom seven demons had gone out, and Joanna, the wife of Herod's steward Chuza, and Susanna, and many others, who provided for them out of their resources.

A friend of mine earns little from his work as a film critic and worries frequently about money. His partner works, too, but he feels, as the man of the family, that he should be the 'breadwinner'.

Jesus seems to have had no such anxieties. We know that Judas was the disciples' treasurer (he 'had the common purse', John 13:29), but where did the contents of that purse come from? Today's story suggests a regular source: well-off women who followed the itinerant preacher and his raggle-taggle bunch of friends around the country.

Plays and films about Jesus usually include Mary Magdalene, plus Jesus' mother and, perhaps, a story of a woman being healed. Yet the other women, who are actually named, seem mysteriously to disappear from our accounts of the Gospel story. Why is that?

They must have been dynamic and enterprising women to leave their other duties and travel around with this band of 'religious nutcases'. Some may have been businesswomen like Lydia (Acts 16:14). Most of them probably had wealthy husbands; they certainly must have had tolerant ones!

This is our first sight of Mary Magdalene and all we learn is that she had had 'seven demons' cast out from her. In modern terms, we might suspect that she had a severe mental illness, which Jesus miraculously healed. No wonder she wanted to follow him. I've suffered depression for over 35 years and have many online friends with depression or more severe mental health problems. I would certainly follow someone who healed me with a few words.

Incidentally, this passage is the best evidence to counter the tradition that Mary Magdalene was a prostitute. If she had been, would Jesus have been happy to live off her earnings? I rather doubt it.

Prayer
Pray for anyone you know who struggles with mental health difficulties.

VZ

Stand up for Jesus

Now he was teaching in one of the synagogues on the sabbath. And just then there appeared a woman with a spirit that had crippled her for eighteen years. She was bent over and was quite unable to stand up straight. When Jesus saw her, he called her over and said, 'Woman, you are set free from your ailment.'… Immediately she stood up straight and began praising God. But the leader of the synagogue… kept saying to the crowd, 'There are six days on which work ought to be done; come on those days and be cured, and not on the sabbath day.' But the Lord answered… 'You hypocrites! Does not each of you on the sabbath untie his ox or his donkey from the manger, and lead it away to give it water? And ought not this woman, a daughter of Abraham whom Satan bound for eighteen long years, be set free from this bondage on the sabbath day?'

Mary Magdalene disappears from our view between that brief glimpse in Luke and her appearance at the crucifixion. So, for a few days, we'll focus on her fellow women of the Gospels and how they encountered Jesus.

Today's passage is my favourite Gospel story. For me, it is a summing up of what we know about how Jesus treated women. We need to remember that, for pious Jewish men, it was forbidden to talk to a woman, even your wife, outside your home. One group, nicknamed the Bruised or Bleeding Pharisees, walked around with eyes lowered all the time, in case they accidentally saw a woman and were caused to have lustful thoughts (that's why they bled—they didn't look where they were going!).

Older translations have Jesus saying, 'Woman, you are free of your infirmity.' I like that because a traditional view of women often sees us as being in some way naturally 'infirm'—'the weaker sex'. Jesus not only scandalously summons this woman to him, he tells her to stand up straight: she becomes a person of dignity, able to look others in the eye again.

The title 'Daughter of Abraham' was quite unknown: it looks as though Jesus invented it. This woman is a pattern for all people, especially women, who grow into their real worth in Jesus.

Reflection

Do you feel that you are growing into your full stature in Christ?

VZ

JOHN 4:5–10 (NRSV, ABRIDGED)

Well connected?

So he came to a Samaritan city called Sychar. Jacob's well was there, and Jesus, tired out by his journey, was sitting by the well. It was about noon. A Samaritan woman came to draw water, and Jesus said to her, 'Give me a drink.' (His disciples had gone to the city to buy food.) The Samaritan woman said to him, 'How is it that you, a Jew, ask a drink of me, a woman of Samaria?' (Jews do not share things in common with Samaritans.) Jesus answered her, 'If you knew the gift of God, and who it is that is saying to you, "Give me a drink," you would have asked him, and he would have given you living water.'

Sadly, it is often our nearest neighbours, culturally and geographically, to whom we are most hostile. Samaritans were the remnant of the northern kingdom of Israel. They had intermarried with their Assyrian conquerors and their Jewish faith had absorbed elements of pagan religions. To the Jews, they were 'dirty heretics' and even to share a cup with one was to contaminate yourself.

So, why is Jesus, a rabbi, a holy man, asking for water from a Samaritan woman, who comes to the well in the midday heat when no one else does, presumably because of her bad reputation? When the disciples return from their shopping, they are so shocked that they dare not even ask (v. 27).

Social rules don't seem to bother Jesus much. A hymn we sing often in my church has the lines 'Race and class and sex and language, Such are barriers he derides.' Notice that it is not her need but his own that draws him to the well. Thirsty and tired, he is prepared to let even the 'lowest of the low' minister to him. Also, the potential he sees in her leads her to become the first woman evangelist: 'Come and see a man who told me everything I have ever done! He cannot be the Messiah, can he?' (v. 29).

When we minister to 'the least and the last', we often find that they give us far more than we ever give them.

Reflection

'And the king will answer them, "Truly I tell you, just as you did it to one of the least of these who are members of my family, you did it to me"' (Matthew 25:40).

VZ

Outcasts

From there he set out and went away to the region of Tyre. He entered a house and did not want anyone to know he was there. Yet he could not escape notice, but a woman whose little daughter had an unclean spirit immediately heard about him, and she came and bowed down at his feet. Now the woman was a Gentile, of Syrophoenician origin. She begged him to cast the demon out of her daughter. He said to her, 'Let the children be fed first, for it is not fair to take the children's food and throw it to the dogs.' But she answered him, 'Sir, even the dogs under the table eat the children's crumbs.' Then he said to her, 'For saying that, you may go—the demon has left your daughter.' So she went home, found the child lying on the bed, and the demon gone.

This passage was the text of the first sermon I ever preached, to a large and well-known church. I was very nervous! As the service was part of a weekend on gender issues, I concentrated on the woman's status as an outsider, excluded from God's chosen people. (I was not a mother then; nowadays, as the mother of a child with special needs, I might have focused on her own needs as a mother.) I suggested that she did, in fact as well as in appearance, change Jesus' mind about the scope of his mission. After all, Jesus as a human being was not omniscient and needed to learn and grow as we all do (see Luke 2:40).

From this, I made the point that, in our churches, there are also people who are outsiders, who feel excluded from God's people, and that, actually, these are just the people we need to listen to. Afterwards, as I returned to my seat, I heard an old lady say to her neighbour, 'This church is going from bad to worse'! At coffee, though, I was approached and thanked by a man who had not dared to confess his homosexuality and he told me that this was the first time he'd ever felt included in that church.

Jesus' attitude to women in the Gospels gives hope to all who, for whatever reason, feel like second-class citizens.

Prayer

Pray for all who feel excluded.

VZ

JOHN 8:3–11 (NRSV, ABRIDGED)

Rough justice

The scribes and the Pharisees brought a woman who had been caught in adultery; and making her stand before all of them, they said to him, 'Teacher, this woman was caught in the very act of committing adultery. Now in the law Moses commanded us to stone such women. Now what do you say?'... When they kept on questioning him, he... said to them, 'Let anyone among you who is without sin be the first to throw a stone at her.'... When they heard it, they went away, one by one, beginning with the elders; and Jesus was left alone with the woman standing before him. Jesus... said to her, 'Woman, where are they? Has no one condemned you?' She said, 'No one, sir.' And Jesus said, 'Neither do I condemn you. Go your way, and from now on do not sin again.'

Much of my misspent youth was misspent reading Victorian novels. In stories such as George Eliot's *Adam Bede* or Thomas Hardy's *Tess of the D'Urbervilles*, there is a clear hierarchy of sins. Sexual sin is worse than any other and sexual sin committed by a woman is worse than the same sin committed by a man.

It seems that this double standard did not originate with the Victorians. The religious leaders here seem to have conveniently forgotten that the Law prescribes that both the man and the woman should be punished (Leviticus 20.10). As the woman was caught in the very act, there could be no doubt about who the man was, yet they blame only the woman.

Blaming women for men's sins has a long and dishonourable heritage. Medieval Christians were very fond of portraying women as insatiably lustful creatures, waiting to trip men up at every turn. I am afraid bits of Proverbs read rather that way as well (see ch. 7), though Proverbs does also portray divine wisdom as a woman (see ch. 8).

Jesus will have no part in this uneven meting out of justice. I wonder what he was writing in the sand before he answered the woman's accusers. Could it be the Law from Leviticus? In any case, he does not see sins as being graded from minor to major, nor women as temptresses. His response to sin is wise, shrewd and compassionate; may ours be likewise.

Reflection
'Do not judge, so that you may not be judged' (Matthew 7:1).

VZ

Contamination?

As he went, the crowds pressed in on him. Now there was a woman who had been suffering from haemorrhages for twelve years; and though she had spent all she had on physicians, no one could cure her. She came up behind him and touched the fringe of his clothes, and immediately her haemorrhage stopped. Then Jesus asked, 'Who touched me?… I noticed that power had gone out from me.' When the woman saw that she could not remain hidden, she came trembling; and falling down before him, she declared in the presence of all the people why she had touched him, and how she had been immediately healed. He said to her, 'Daughter, your faith has made you well; go in peace.'

A Jewish journalist decided recently, as an experiment, that he would attempt for a whole year to live according to biblical laws (although I don't think he stoned any adulterers) and then write a book about it. His wife wasn't quite so keen on the project as he refused to sit anywhere where she had sat while having her period!

Menstruation was regarded in biblical times as making a woman unclean, so she had to have a ritual bath to cleanse her at the end of her period. This woman's continual haemorrhages would have made her unclean all the time, unable to mix in society and even unable to sleep with her husband. For her to touch the fringe of Jesus' prayer shawl would have, in turn, made him unclean. No wonder she was trembling when he called her out of the crowd.

With a few affirming words, though, Jesus here demolishes the entire system of purity and impurity that was the structure of religion at the time. This system impacted particularly severely on women. Not only menstruation but also childbirth made them 'impure', so women's natural bodily processes made them unfit to be with company for a large proportion of their lives. Jesus tells his disciples that we are made clean or unclean not by what goes into or comes out of our bodies but by what comes out of our hearts (Matthew 15:17–18).

Reflection

'So God created humankind in his image… male and female he created them… God saw everything that he had made, and indeed, it was very good' (Genesis 1:27, 31).

VZ

Something to say

One of the Pharisees asked Jesus to eat with him, and he went into the Pharisee's house and took his place at the table. And a woman in the city, who was a sinner, having learned that he was eating in the Pharisee's house, brought an alabaster jar of ointment. She stood behind him at his feet, weeping, and began to bathe his feet with her tears and to dry them with her hair. Then she continued kissing his feet and anointing them with the ointment. Now when the Pharisee who had invited him saw it, he said to himself, 'If this man were a prophet, he would have known who and what kind of woman this is who is touching him—that she is a sinner.' Jesus spoke up and said to him, 'Simon, I have something to say to you.'

'Simon, I have something to say to you'—or, as I put it in a poem on this passage, 'There is some educating to be done.'

The tradition that Mary Magdalene was a prostitute stems mainly from this passage, which is often confused with other stories of women anointing Jesus (for example, Mark 14:3–9). In particular, it is linked with the story of Mary of Bethany anointing Jesus' feet (John 11:1–2). If anyone should be labelled a prostitute, the evidence points more to Martha's sister, who is quite different from Mary Magdalene. In fact, it is impossible to disentangle the various anointing stories and, in any case, this version does not specify what this woman's sins were. We do know, however, that prostitutes followed Jesus, who forgave their sins (Matthew 21:31).

In response to Simon's criticism, Jesus tells the story of two debtors who were forgiven their debts (Luke 7:41–43). Asked which loved the creditor more, Simon concedes that it was the one who was forgiven the larger debt. Love, Jesus suggests, 'covers a multitude of sins' (1 Peter 4:8).

I wonder what would happen if a disreputable woman came into a Christian meeting and started to wash the speaker's feet, dry them with her hair and spray perfume on them. I think we might be just as shocked. Jesus' forgiveness and his respect for all women are still revolutionary.

Prayer

Pray for the ministry of those who work with vulnerable or abused women.

VZ

A tutorial session

Now as they went on their way, he entered a certain village, where a woman named Martha welcomed him into her home. She had a sister named Mary, who sat at the Lord's feet and listened to what he was saying. But Martha was distracted by her many tasks; so she came to him and asked, 'Lord, do you not care that my sister has left me to do all the work by myself? Tell her then to help me.' But the Lord answered her, 'Martha, Martha, you are worried and distracted by many things; there is need of only one thing. Mary has chosen the better part, which will not be taken away from her.'

Do you know, I have just noticed something that I never noticed before about this story. When Jesus says that Mary's job will not be taken away from her, is he suggesting that Martha's will? Does that mean there's no housework in heaven?

Seriously, though, this story is a lot more radical than is often realized. To 'sit at the feet of' a religious teacher was to be his disciple and pupil—Paul sat at the feet of Gamaliel (Acts 22:3) and quotes this as part of his rabbinical credentials. Women just did not do that sort of thing. Mary is the equivalent here of the first women who ever went to university and her position must have caused as much scandal as they did.

Martha's occupation is firmly within the sphere that tradition has always allocated to women: cooking, cleaning, hospitality in general. I'm sure she was an ace cook and generous host, but Jesus does not (somewhat disappointingly, in fact) commend her for it. Indeed, he lightly pokes fun at her attempt to be a domestic goddess, but praises Mary for prioritizing her religious education over helping Martha.

So, this is not just a story about not worrying or staying close to Jesus. It is a story about a whole new world opening up for women. I don't know if Mary of Bethany is the patron saint of women theologians, but she ought to be—perhaps of all theologians.

Reflection

Does your church open all ministries to women or restrict some to men only? What justification does it give for its choice? Do you agree with its stance?

VZ

MATTHEW 27:55–61 (NRSV, ABRIDGED)

Faithful followers

Many women were also there, looking on from a distance; they had followed Jesus from Galilee and had provided for him. Among them were Mary Magdalene, and Mary the mother of James and Joseph, and the mother of the sons of Zebedee. When it was evening, there came a rich man from Arimathea, named Joseph, who... went to Pilate and asked for the body of Jesus; then Pilate ordered it to be given to him. So Joseph took the body and wrapped it in a clean linen cloth and laid it in his own new tomb... He then rolled a great stone to the door of the tomb and went away. Mary Magdalene and the other Mary were there, sitting opposite the tomb.

We are sometimes told by preachers that all the disciples abandoned Jesus (Matthew 26:56). That is only partly true: the women stayed, even if it was 'at a distance'. They might well have stayed nearer if they hadn't had to run the gauntlet of rough Roman soldiers.

At last, Mary Magdalene comes back into view and we learn that she has followed Jesus right to the end. The parallel passage in Mark (15:47) tells us that 'Mary Magdalene and Mary the mother of Joses saw where the body was laid'. Reading these words, I get the strong impression that this verse is a 'witness statement', providing evidence against any story that Jesus was not really dead but was spirited away to be revived later.

This makes the two Marys members of a very select group: those who are, in the words of Acts 1:22, 'a witness with us'. Considering that the testimony of a woman was not legally valid in court, the Gospels are doing something very unexpected when they record these women's testimony.

How might church history—or, indeed, political history—have been different if leaders had listened more to the testimony of women? Maybe we would not have had so many wars, including religious wars, if women had refused to send their sons to fight. Women are just as fallible and apt to be mistaken as men are, but we do tend to notice the human dimensions of events. Jesus, as we shall see, chose women to be the first witnesses of his resurrection.

Prayer

Pray for anyone you know who is suffering from a bereavement.

VZ

Afraid to believe

When the sabbath was over, Mary Magdalene, and Mary the mother of James, and Salome bought spices, so that they might go and anoint him... They had been saying to one another, 'Who will roll away the stone for us from the entrance to the tomb?' When they looked up, they saw that the stone, which was very large, had already been rolled back. As they entered the tomb, they saw a young man, dressed in a white robe, sitting on the right side; and they were alarmed. But he said to them, 'Do not be alarmed; you are looking for Jesus of Nazareth, who was crucified. He has been raised; he is not here. Look, there is the place they laid him. But go, tell his disciples and Peter that he is going ahead of you to Galilee; there you will see him, just as he told you.' So they went out and fled from the tomb, for terror and amazement had seized them; and they said nothing to anyone, for they were afraid.

This, the most reliable ending of Mark's Gospel, may be the earliest account of the resurrection. Scholars disagree about why Mark's account ends so abruptly and, indeed, our modern translations all include verses 9–20, which are in later manuscripts, telling of various people's meetings with the risen Jesus (including Mary Magdalene's).

There is certainly something disturbing about being left with the women too afraid to speak. Yet, there is also a realism and a challenge in this inconclusive end. There is realism, because how would you feel if you went to tend your mentor's grave and found an empty tomb and a strange messenger? It was brave of the women to visit the tomb at all, knowing that it was guarded. There are many places in our world today where it is dangerous for grieving women to visit the graves of their families and friends who have been slaughtered in communal violence.

There is challenge because we, the readers, are in the same position that the women were at this point: we have not seen the risen Jesus; we have to take someone else's word for it that he is risen. So this ending challenges us: will you believe, on the word of those who were closest to him?

Reflect

'He has been raised.' What difference does that make to us?

VZ

LUKE 24:5–11 (NRSV)

An old wives' tale?

The women were terrified and bowed their faces to the ground, but the men said to them, 'Why do you look for the living among the dead? He is not here, but has risen. Remember how he told you, while he was still in Galilee, that the Son of Man must be handed over to sinners, and be crucified, and on the third day rise again.' Then they remembered his words, and returning from the tomb, they told all this to the eleven and to all the rest. Now it was Mary Magdalene, Joanna, Mary the mother of James, and the other women with them who told this to the apostles. But these words seemed to them an idle tale, and they did not believe them.

Of the many derogatory things that have been said about women through the ages, one of the most frequent is that women imagine things and elaborate their accounts of events, so that you cannot rely on a woman's word.

Matthew's and Luke's accounts of the resurrection are fuller and more detailed than Mark's—Luke even has not one, but two 'men in white' (v. 4) at the tomb (whichever it was, it would be foolish therefore to conclude that there were none at all). What the accounts agree on is the prominence of the women in these events: whether it was Mary Magdalene on her own, 'the women' or those on the list of names we have here.

It's difficult for us to take on board how striking, even shocking, that would have been to the first readers or hearers of these stories. When a woman's testimony was automatically thought to be invalid, what on earth was Jesus thinking of, entrusting the news of his rising to women? They were sure not to be believed.

Perhaps, though, he knew exactly what he was doing. In the new world that was being inaugurated by his resurrection, the prophecy of Joel was about to be fulfilled: 'your sons and your daughters shall prophesy… Even on the male and female slaves… I will pour out my spirit' (Joel 2:28–29 and again in Acts 2:17–18). In the age of the Spirit, distinctions of class and gender are irrelevant: God can speak through anyone.

Reflection

When have you heard God's voice from an unexpected source?

VZ

Still grieving

Early on the first day of the week, while it was still dark, Mary Magdalene came to the tomb and saw that the stone had been removed from the tomb. So she ran and went to Simon Peter and the other disciple, the one whom Jesus loved, and said to them, 'They have taken the Lord out of the tomb, and we do not know where they have laid him.' Then Peter and the other disciple set out and went towards the tomb... Then the disciples returned to their homes. But Mary stood weeping outside the tomb.

We're sticking with the resurrection—not only because the women are so prominent in the various accounts but also because each account gives us a different angle on the story. If there is any 'spin' in John's account, it is perhaps that the men have a more prominent place. He tells us how Peter and the disciple 'whom Jesus loved' (maybe John himself) ran to the tomb (vv. 2, 4–7), where the wrappings were lying folded with no body in them, and at least one of them 'saw and believed' (v. 8).

For Mary, though (as for Thomas later), the evidence of the empty tomb alone was not enough. What was she waiting for? Perhaps she didn't know herself. Out of breath (she had run twice as far as Peter and John), confused, afraid, maybe she just needed time to process the extraordinary turn of events. It's not so easy, when an overwhelming grief has turned to a tentative, hardly understood prospect of joy, to let go of the desperate feelings that bereavement has produced. We need to do our grieving properly before we can embark on a new and different life, with a different focus.

Yet, it's precisely because Mary stayed, still carrying her now useless spices, that she was able to have the encounter with the living Jesus we will read about tomorrow. She will move from desperation to hope, from hardly believed angels' accounts of Jesus' resurrection to a personal experience of her living Redeemer.

Christians are sometimes keen to move people on quickly from difficult experiences and may push them, inappropriately, into seeing events positively. Sometimes, however, it is in the midst of our grief that we encounter the living Jesus.

Prayer

Pray for anyone you know who has lost their sense of God's presence.

VZ

Joy comes with the morning

As [Mary] wept, she bent over to look into the tomb; and she saw two angels in white, sitting where the body of Jesus had been lying, one at the head and the other at the feet. They said to her, 'Woman, why are you weeping?' She said to them, 'They have taken away my Lord, and I do not know where they have laid him.' When she had said this, she turned around and saw Jesus standing there, but she did not know that it was Jesus. Jesus said to her, 'Woman, why are you weeping? Whom are you looking for?' Supposing him to be the gardener, she said to him, 'Sir, if you have carried him away, tell me where you have laid him, and I will take him away.' Jesus said to her, 'Mary!'

'They have taken away my Lord'—what great desolation those few words express. I suspect many of us have felt like this at times. Some will have had a personal bereavement. For some, as in the cyclone in Burma or the earthquake in China, which are recent events as I write, there will not be a visible body to care for. Others are living with a sense that the God who once seemed so close does not speak to them any more. This, too, is a kind of bereavement.

Mary is not one to give up, though, even when all seems lost. Blinded by tears or for some other reason, she does not recognize the living Lord. Yet, she is still ready to catch at any chance of serving her Master, if only by taking charge of his corpse.

Then it comes, the familiar voice, speaking her name. It is almost impossible to imagine her joy—not only because Jesus is risen but also because he speaks personally to her; he is the same Jesus by whom she has always been affirmed. Although day has already dawned, this must have been a true, inner dawn for her.

In the context of the time, it is truly amazing that the first appearance of the risen Jesus is to this woman with such a chequered history. He cannot, then, be far from any of us.

Prayer

'My soul waits for the Lord more than those who watch for the morning' (Psalm 130:6).

VZ

The apostle Mary?

Jesus said to her, 'Mary!' She turned and said to him in Hebrew, 'Rabbouni!' (which means Teacher). Jesus said to her, 'Do not hold on to me, because I have not yet ascended to the Father. But go to my brothers and say to them, "I am ascending to my Father and your Father, to my God and your God."' Mary Magdalene went and announced to the disciples, 'I have seen the Lord'; and she told them that he had said these things to her.

One of my favourite paintings of all time is Fra Angelico's gentle portrayal of this meeting in a garden, painted on the wall of a monk's cell at the monastery of San Marco outside Florence. Such paintings of this scene are normally titled *Noli me tangere*, ('Do not touch me'), echoing Jesus' words to Mary.

Why was Mary not allowed to hold on to the risen Jesus? I don't think it was because he was some sort of insubstantial ghost—other Bible passages show him eating and drinking (see Luke 24:38–43). I suspect the clue is in his statement, 'I have not yet ascended to the Father.' The mysterious form in which Jesus appeared to his disciples after his resurrection was only for a small group of people to see and relate to. To have held on to this physical presence would have been to hold on to something that was passing. The ascended Jesus, however, can meet with all of us and speak to all of us.

Sometimes, indeed, we may long for something more immediate and physically present. That is the time to turn to our fellow Christians, who are God's hands and feet (and arms, for hugs) to us. That, in fact, is what Mary does: rather than wanting to stay in the garden and feast her eyes on her beloved Jesus, she obeys him and takes the message to her fellow disciples (though, as we have read elsewhere, they didn't necessarily believe her at once).

Because of this message with which she was entrusted, Mary was known in the early Church as 'the apostle to the apostles'. There could hardly be a greater title. All this for a woman who had been a mentally ill outcast from society!

Reflection

Which women, alive or dead, have helped you to meet Jesus?

VZ

A taste of Leviticus

I knew next to nothing about Leviticus before I began to write these notes. Now I still know next to nothing but the next is just over there on the other side of nothing. Thank God for the experts—and that, I can assure you, is not blasphemy.

Leviticus covers the period after the people of Israel were rescued from slavery in Egypt. Moses had led them across the desert to Mount Sinai, where God pronounced his law and made a covenant with the people. Next, Moses is to receive further instruction on the best way for Israel to maintain its special relationship with the Lord.

The book is a long one, but it divides fairly neatly into two parts. The first 17 chapters are to do with the complicated rituals of sacrifice and establishing a right relationship with God. We might sum up this half up with the words of the first commandment: 'Love the Lord your God with all your heart, soul, mind and strength.'

Chapters 18 to 27 centre on another commandment: 'Love your neighbour as yourself.' These chapters call Israel to be holy in every area of their practical lives and are sometimes known as the 'holiness code'.

There it is, then. Those are some of the things that I have learned, but I wish I knew more. Leviticus is a very complex and intense piece of work, filled with a sort of urgent drive towards making sure that not a single detail needed to establish a right relationship between God and his people has been omitted.

Will we recognize Jesus in the God we seem to encounter in this book? That is a question I have asked more than once in these notes. The complexity of the sacrificial rituals, the total lack of compromise, the swift and apparently merciless execution of Aaron's two sons when they went a flame too far, the exclusion of any less than physically perfect individuals from the priesthood—all these things are difficult to understand. Yet, I think those of you who are unfamiliar with Leviticus will be intrigued and fascinated by the parallels between this distant culture and the faith we know. Jesus has made the final sacrifice so that we can enjoy the extraordinary freedom that is possible when the law of God is written on our hearts. Here is my taste of Leviticus. I hope you enjoy it.

Adrian Plass

LEVITICUS 1:1–4 (TNIV)

No rubbish for God

The Lord called to Moses and spoke to him from the tent of meeting. He said, 'Speak to the Israelites and say to them: "When you bring an offering to the Lord, bring as your offering an animal from either the herd or the flock. If the offering is a burnt offering from the herd, you are to offer a male without defect. You must present it at the entrance to the tent of meeting so that you may be acceptable to the Lord. You are to lay your hand on the head of the burnt offering, and it will be accepted on your behalf to make atonement for you."'

God is not interested in our old rubbish, neither an animal with one leg and no flesh on its bones, nor scraps of time and odd bits of loose change that we can give away without any sense of loss. The book of Malachi takes up this theme again and our modern Church would do well to consider the significance of these stern injunctions.

A man I know started giving regularly to a project in Malaysia. All was well until he wrote to the project leaders asking them to undertake a task for him in that country. They couldn't help for one reason or another and my friend was furious. 'I've sent them so much money,' he complained, 'and now that I want a little favour from them they say they can't help. It's not fair!'

I felt a passing sympathy for my friend, but he had never explained to the Malaysians that he was not actually giving them the money, he was selling it to them. From his point of view, the people in that project were in his debt. His offering was a bit of a lame and manky old goat, wouldn't you say?

The bottom line seems to be that a sacrifice has to be a sacrifice. OK, that may be an obvious thing to say, but let's not kid ourselves. Many of our so-called gifts to God are the equivalent of those ghastly products of the 1970s that infest the shelves of so many charity shops and were never really wanted in the first place.

Be honest and either give nothing or hand over the best you've got. That's what God wants.

Prayer

Teach me how to stop messing about and be truly generous, Lord.

AP

LEVITICUS 5:11–13 (TNIV, ABRIDGED)

Whatever you can afford

If... [the guilty person] cannot afford two doves or two young pigeons, they are to bring as an offering for their sin a tenth of an ephah of the finest flour for a sin offering. They must not put oil or incense on it, because it is a sin offering. They are to bring it to the priest, who shall take a handful of it as a memorial portion and burn it on the altar on top of the food offerings presented to the Lord. It is a sin offering. In this way the priest will make atonement for them for any of these sins they have committed, and they will be forgiven.

The opening verse of this passage reminds us that God has never discriminated against the poor in favour of the wealthy. His approval rests on those who make an offering that is extravagant according to their individual means, whether it is an offering to atone for sin or a gift to the Church. The widow who gave her mite in the New Testament (Mark 12:41–44) is an example of this openhandedness. So is my friend Paul.

Paul is one of the most charmingly loyal people you could hope to meet. Knowing him has been a gift from God. He has lived in institutions for most of his life and has access to no more than £3.50 each week.

In our sitting room there is a little enamelled box into which Paul puts money every time he visits. He passionately wants to help needy people. Recently he has decided to make a gift to Toybox, a charity working with street children in Latin America. When his savings amount to ten pounds, we shall write a cheque and send it off for him. Paul would give all his money if allowed. We usually suggest that he puts in 50 pence or a pound on each occasion. The ten pounds will soon accumulate.

Paul has less cash than anyone I know and some might regard him as a very unimportant person indeed. The reality is that Paul (and many other people) will get a surprise when he arrives in heaven. In addition to his sins being wiped out and forgotten, he will be extremely famous and he will be a millionaire.

Reflection

Will we realize too late how rich we might have been?

AP

Washed and wrapped for business

Moses said to the assembly, 'This is what the Lord has command-ed to be done.' Then Moses brought Aaron and his sons forward and washed them with water. He put the tunic on Aaron, tied the sash round him, clothed him with the robe and put the ephod on him. He also fastened the ephod with a decorative waistband, which he tied round him. He placed the breastpiece on him and put the Urim and Thummim in the breastpiece. Then he placed the tur-ban on Aaron's head and set the gold plate, the sacred emblem, on the front of it, as the Lord commanded Moses.

This really is extraordinary, isn't it? It reminds me of one of James Herriot's stories of life as a country vet in Yorkshire. The young Herriot was persuaded by a grizzled old vet-erinary practitioner to wear a ridiculously confining rubber calv-ing suit and cap at a local farm. To the amusement of onlookers, it transpired that the role of this amazingly attired person was sim-ply to pass a pessary to the senior vet.

Here is Aaron, dressed up like something between a pantomime villain and a character from *Star Wars*—and this was only the begin-ning. After the sons had been washed and Aaron had donned his complicated gear, they all had to be marked with sacrificial blood on their right ears, hands and toes. Then they were sprinkled, robes and all, with oil and blood. Finally, they were to cook the meat used in the offering, eat some of it, burn the rest and spend seven days by the entrance to the Tent of Meeting.

So why was all this dressing up and sprinkling and washing and eating so important? Perhaps it has something to do with the need for Aaron and his sons to be totally immersed, absorbed and bound up in the important task that lay before them. Human beings are so fickle and distractible. The complexity of the ceremonial detail was like a net, holding them fast until the job was done, and done properly.

We don't have to do all that fid-dling around nowadays, but how much of ourselves do we voluntar-ily throw into the tasks that God gives us? Freedom feels like hard work sometimes.

Prayer

Father, make us clean and presentable, ready to give everything for you.

AP

Authorized fire

Then Aaron lifted his hands towards the people and blessed them. And having sacrificed the sin offering, the burnt offering and the fellowship offering, he stepped down. Moses and Aaron then went into the tent of meeting. When they came out, they blessed the people; and the glory of the Lord appeared to all the people. Fire came out from the presence of the Lord and consumed the burnt offering and the fat portions on the altar. And when all the people saw it, they shouted for joy and fell face down.

Here we are at the end of the long and complicated process involved in the ordination of Aaron and his sons as priests. Bulls, goats, rams and calves have been prepared and offered, all in a meticulously ceremonial fashion, to atone for the sins of the new priests and the nation of Israel. God has promised that, if all is done well, he will appear to them and show his glory. Now the moment has come. Suddenly, as Moses and Aaron come out of the tent of meeting and bless the people, supernatural fire roars into life, consuming the sacrifices and filling the people with an exhilarating mixture of joy and terror.

Isn't it good when God turns up? Of course, he's always there, but you know what I mean. When times have been hard and the road has been rough and you've tried, not very successfully, to do the right thing and you're ready to give up, it's fantastic when the authentic fire of God blazes into your life, turning all that you offer to ashes, but leaving you quivering with relief because he has come and heaven has once more swept reassuringly across the earth and everything is all right.

Doesn't happen often, does it? Why not? I wonder if it is connected with the casual inconsistency with which we conduct our spiritual journeys. I remember John Wimber obediently preaching healing for a year, during which time nobody was healed, and then seeing the power of God working in the bodies of countless people. I have a deep yearning to see the fire of God. I'm just not sure if I can keep my feet firmly on a path that seems very wearisome at times.

Prayer

Come, Lord Jesus, this morning, this evening. Now. Give us courage.

AP

LEVITICUS 10:1–5 (TNIV)

Unauthorized fire

Aaron's sons Nadab and Abihu took their censers, put fire in them and added incense; and they offered unauthorized fire before the Lord, contrary to his command. So fire came out from the presence of the Lord and consumed them, and they died before the Lord. Moses then said to Aaron, 'This is what the Lord spoke of when he said: "Among those who approach me I will be proved holy; in the sight of all the people I will be honoured."' Aaron remained silent. Moses summoned Mishael and Elzaphan, sons of Aaron's uncle Uzziel, and said to them, 'Come here; carry your cousins outside the camp, away from the front of the sanctuary.' So they came and carried them, still in their tunics, outside the camp, as Moses ordered.

Oh dear. In the opening chapter of Malachi, God rebukes his priests for offering 'useless fires' on the altar (1:10). When will we learn that God never, never, never appreciates the fabricated spirituality of those who get carried away with purely human excitement and ambition?

What a sad story this is. The Bible surprises me sometimes with a verse so poignantly vivid that it brings tears to my eyes. Another example appears in chapter 14 of Matthew's Gospel. When Jesus heard about the death of his cousin John, he 'withdrew by boat privately to a solitary place' (v. 13). Of course, the crowds soon found him. Jesus never had much time to himself.

Here, Aaron remains silent. Overwhelmed by grief at the death of his sons, what else can he do? There is nothing to say. Nahab and Abihu got it wrong. They tried to make God happen and God didn't like it. How sad to learn that they were carried off 'still in their tunics'—colourful symbols of a future that had looked so bright and successful.

Talk about a spiritual boot camp, eh? What a tough course. No compromise, no second chances. My way or the highway, thus saith the Lord. Clearly there was a need for absolute purity in the priesthood and I expect God knew what he was doing…

However we react to this sorry tale, one lesson is clear. Don't try to make God happen. He doesn't like it. It won't work. The fire has to come from him.

Prayer

Let it be your fire, Lord, not mine.

AP

Why all the fuss?

The Lord said to Moses, 'These are the regulations for any diseased person at the time of their ceremonial cleansing, when they are brought to the priest: the priest is to go outside the camp and examine them. If they have been healed of their defiling skin disease, the priest shall order that two live clean birds and some cedar wood, scarlet yarn and hyssop be brought for the person to be cleansed. Then the priest shall order that one of the birds be killed over fresh water in a clay pot. He is then to take the live bird and dip it, together with the cedar wood, the scarlet yarn and the hyssop, into the blood of the bird that was killed over the fresh water.'

This is only the beginning. Read on to verse 18 and see what an incredibly complicated business this is. If I had been one of the diseased, I might have given up halfway through and settled for staying diseased and having a quieter life. I suppose you have to bear in mind that sickness and sin were related in the minds of the Israelites. Centuries later, Jesus was to show that this was not invariably the case, as his encounter with the blind man in John 9 demonstrates (see especially vv. 2–3). Having said that, his healings were frequently preceded by forgiveness of sins, so, as usual, we cannot establish a comfortably fixed rule and adhere to it.

What do we make of all this? How can we equate this God, who had his priests interminably fussing about clothes and animals and grain and goodness knows what, with the God we meet in Jesus, described in Colossians as 'the image of the invisible God' (1:15)?

You will not be surprised to learn that I cannot adequately answer that question. I have tried before and failed. What I can do is retreat to a truth that means much more than any question, however challenging. There is something about Jesus, something that sings to me, something extraordinarily ordinary, purely divine—something I trust. He liked friends and fire and food and wine and treats and kindness and generosity. If he is the image of God, then I will happily follow him. For now, the questions can wait.

Prayer

Whatever the sickness in us,
bring healing, Lord.

AP

Now we have Jesus

'It is a day of sabbath rest, and you must deny yourselves; it is a lasting ordinance. The priest who is anointed and ordained to succeed his father as high priest is to make atonement. He is to put on the sacred linen garments and make atonement for the Most Holy Place, for the tent of meeting and the altar, and for the priests and all the members of the community. This is to be a lasting ordinance for you: atonement is to be made once a year for all the sins of the Israelites.' And it was done, as the Lord commanded Moses.

This passage suggests half an answer to the hard question I asked in yesterday's reading. It is speaking about the Day of Atonement, an annual event in which Aaron the high priest made sacrifices for the sins of the people. The Israelites were expected to fast and show sorrow for their sins. It was a solemn festival involving none of the celebration and joyful dancing that occurred in such festivals as the feast of Tabernacles. Nowadays it is called Yom Kippur and is one of the holiest days in the Jewish year.

Christians need no Day of Atonement or any long, complicated rituals or burnt sacrifices. The Day of Atonement is fulfilled in the death of Jesus—he gave his own body as a sacrifice for the sins of the whole world. He is both the perfect high priest and the perfect sacrifice.

Finally, after thousands of years of obfuscation, we have something approaching a clear picture of the nature of God. When C.S. Lewis read the translation of the New Testament by J.B. Phillips, he said that it was as though a familiar painting had been cleaned and become properly visible at last. I don't know why it took so long for the portrait of our heavenly Father to lose its patina of ritual and complexity. Who knows what goes on behind the scenes? Let's decide, though, to be grateful that we are allowed access to the amazingly unvarnished truth that is summed up in John's Gospel (3:16): 'For God so loved the world that he gave his one and only Son, that whoever believes in him shall not perish but have eternal life.'

Reflection

We have something to celebrate. It's all been done—we're in!

AP

Stay clean

Do not defile yourselves in any of these ways, because this is how the nations that I am going to drive out before you became defiled. Even the land was defiled; so I punished it for its sin, and the land vomited out its inhabitants. But you must keep my decrees and my laws. The native-born and the foreigners residing among you must not do any of these detestable things, for all these things were done by the people who lived in the land before you, and the land became defiled. And if you defile the land, it will vomit you out as it vomited out the nations that were before you.

These verses appear towards the end of a chapter that is exclusively concerned with the categorization of improper sexual relationships. More than 20 are listed. There is a much simpler way to understand these instructions: have sex only with your wife or husband and you will not be vomited out by the land (an unpleasant-sounding fate, to say the least).

I have always loved 'clean'. As a child, I probably read far too much Victorian literature. I wanted human beings to be filled with honour and integrity and unswerving loyalty to those who are dependent on them. Husbands would love and cherish their wives. Wives would be equally devoted to their husbands. Neither of them would have had sex with any other person, nor would it ever occur to them to consider such a thing. You can laugh if you like, but that was my dream and the yearning to live in a world that is morally clean has never really left me.

Of course, this fantasy is exploded by the briefest excursion into my own inner world. I don't mean that I have an overwhelming desire to rush out and have an affair, but my mind is not pure. I guess nobody's is. What shall we do?

As humbly as possible (we can talk about problems in the humility department another time), we have to accept that our righteousness, our moral perfection, exists only in the risen Jesus—he presents us spotless to his Father. That is truly wonderful, but the child in me still wishes that it could be true down here as well.

Reflection

Vomited out of the land? How? Where? When? What?

AP

Loving the alien

Stand up in the presence of the aged, show respect for the elderly and revere your God. I am the Lord. When foreigners reside among you in your land, do not mistreat them. The foreigners residing among you must be treated as your native-born. Love them as yourself, for you were foreigners in Egypt. I am the Lord your God. Do not use dishonest standards when measuring length, weight or quantity. Use honest scales and honest weights, an honest ephah and an honest hin. I am the Lord your God, who brought you out of Egypt.

If there was ever anything the Israelites were not going to be allowed to forget, it was that God had brought them out of Egypt. This constant repetition is reminiscent of the cry of many frustrated parents over the years: 'After all I've done for you, you turn round and treat me like this.'

I do not believe that God is simply complaining about lack of appreciation. Rather, he is calling the Israelites to exercise their imagination. *De Profundis*, written by Oscar Wilde while imprisoned in Reading Gaol, includes a passage about Jesus and imagination. Jesus, he asserts, could imagine change in people and situations in such a way that supernatural power could bring those imaginings to fruition.

Whatever we think of this perspective, it is true that sympathetic treatment of others is largely dependent on our capacity to picture their predicament and imagine them changing for the better. As a child, my life was changed forever by the astonishing realization that 'Everyone is I'. Each one of us is a star at the centre of life. The Israelites had been appallingly treated in Egypt, their lives filled with back-breaking work and mindless brutality. After leaving the land of their exile, they had endured 40 years of trudging through the desert, longing for their diet of quails and manna to be replaced by the long-promised milk and honey of the promised land. If ever a people was equipped to understand and sympathize with aliens, it was the Israelites.

Don't forget, says God to them and to us, the place you came from and the way in which you were rescued and led to safety. Use your imagination. Help the alien.

Reflection

Your neighbour could be an alien. (No, don't be silly, not that sort of alien!)

AP

Not very PC!

The Lord said to Moses, 'Say to Aaron: "For the generations to come none of your descendants who has a defect may come near to offer the food of his God. No man who has any defect may come near: no man who is blind or lame, disfigured or deformed; no man with a crippled foot or hand, or who is a hunchback or a dwarf, or who has any eye defect, or who has festering or running sores or damaged testicles. No descendant of Aaron the priest who has any defect is to come near to present the food offerings to the Lord. He has a defect; he must not come near to offer the food of his God.'"

This doesn't read comfortably, does it? There wouldn't have been much parading with banners over the issue, though. God never compromised and the threat of being consumed by holy fire like poor old Nadab and Abihu would have prevented most people from making a fuss. Actually, there is no doubt that the idea was not to discriminate against the deformed and disabled, but, as always during this stage in Israel's history, to reflect the purity of God.

Nowadays, God's law is written on our hearts and God lives in us, not in a ceremonial tent somewhere on the local recreation ground. Any person, whether perfect in form or physically afflicted, can be a temple of the Holy Spirit and an ambassador for God. Joni Erickson Tada, injured in a diving accident as a teenager and quadriplegic ever since, has exercised one of the most effective ministries of recent years. None of that stuff matters any more, not in the world of the Spirit.

I know I'm like the boy in the classroom who sticks his hand up to ask awkward questions, but here's a question for God. If he was so bothered about physical perfection in priests, why recruit a man with a speech impediment to head up the operation?

I think that God does whatever needs to be done to move things along at any given moment. That is why it is so dangerous to pluck little bits and pieces out of the Bible and try to use them to prove anything about his nature. Trust God. I know it's not always easy, but we need to try.

Prayer
Lord, thank you for equal rights and opportunities.

AP

117

The way we were?

On the first day you are to take branches from luxuriant trees—from palms, willows and other leafy trees—and rejoice before the Lord your God for seven days. Celebrate this as a festival to the Lord for seven days each year. This is to be a lasting ordinance for the generations to come; celebrate it in the seventh month. Live in temporary shelters for seven days: all native-born Israelites are to live in such shelters so that your descendants will know that I made the Israelites live in temporary shelters when I brought them out of Egypt. I am the Lord your God.

This passage is about the Feast of Tabernacles, which was seven days long, plus a further day of rest and worship. Unlike the solemn Day of Atonement, this was a time of dancing and feasting, to celebrate the end of the harvests. God wants his chosen people to measure and be conscious of positive changes in their lives. In memory of a time when they were forced to live in makeshift desert tents, the Israelites build leafy canopies to live under for seven days. The kids must have loved all this. What fun to prepare the houses and the food and then enjoy the singing and dancing and eating!

The principle is a good one, don't you think? Harvest happens on many levels and needs to be celebrated from time to time. The actual harvest is still important to us, of course. Compared with much of the world, we are rich beyond measure. In terms of food and shelter, education and health, we have an immense amount to be grateful for, however imperfect some of these institutions may appear at times. Then there are the harvests of friendship, family, community, the natural world, work and relaxation. All of these are gifts from God and we do well to thank him for them.

The spiritual harvest is the most important one, of course. It varies for each of us in detail, but we have one central truth in common. A grain of wheat fell to the ground, died and sprang to life again. Jesus is our harvest and the fruits of that harvest are for ever. Worth a few days of dancing and feasting? I think so.

Reflection

If we trust in God, wherever we are and whatever is happening to us is the best that is possible at that time.

AP

The wonder of Jubilee

If any of your own people become poor and sell themselves to you, do not make them work as slaves. They are to be treated as hired workers or temporary residents among you; they are to work for you until the Year of Jubilee. Then they and their children are to be released, and they will go back to their own clans and to the property of their ancestors. Because the Israelites are my servants, whom I brought out of Egypt, they must not be sold as slaves. Do not rule over them ruthlessly, but fear your God.

I have been reminding myself what the Year of Jubilee is all about. This is how I understand it after looking at other people's commentaries. Every 50 years, the Jubilee was to be announced by the blowing of rams' horn trumpets right across the country on the Day of Atonement ('jubilee' actually comes from the Hebrew word for 'ram'). The Day of Atonement was, in any case, a time when harmony was restored between God and his people. Now, in the Year of Jubilee, the peace of God was to permeate the natural world as well.

For those whose families had hit hard times through misfortune or inability to pay debts, this was a wonderful turning point. If they had lost land through these misfortunes, it would be returned to them. Also, families would be relieved of their normal duties so that they could unite and spend time together. Fifty years is an awfully long time, but, in a culture where family and inheritance were hugely significant, it must have acted as a shining beacon to those who had lost property and self-respect.

The Jubilee was based on the fact that the whole of the land actually belonged to God, so was only ever leased to those who worked and lived on it. We should know all about this, of course, as Christians. We tend, though, to pay lip-service to this principle. God owns everything and we are simply stewards of any money or property that is under our control. Do you believe that in your heart? Do I?

Reflection

The rams' horns blow all over this country tomorrow and God declares a Year of Jubilee. Who owns your stuff?

AP

Rewards for obedience

I will look on you with favour and make you fruitful and increase your numbers, and I will keep my covenant with you. You will still be eating last year's harvest when you will have to move it out to make room for the new. I will put my dwelling place among you, and I will not abhor you. I will walk among you and be your God, and you will be my people. I am the Lord your God, who brought you out of Egypt so that you would no longer be slaves to the Egyptians; I broke the bars of your yoke and enabled you to walk with heads held high.

Several months ago, a man approached me after a meeting in which I had been talking about obedience. 'Listening to your talk, Adrian,' he said, 'I reflected on the fact that I've been waiting 20 years for God to make me want to be obedient. When do you think he'll do that?'

I love my job and I'll go on doing it as long as I'm allowed, but sometimes I am gobsmacked by the things people say. This man had listened for an hour and it was as if he had not heard a single word. I wasn't sure what to say.

'Well,' I ventured at last, 'I'm not sure you've quite understood the concept, have you?'

After a short conversation, I realized that part of this chap's problem was a type of poor teaching that has been quite common in evangelical churches in recent decades. It's something to do with personal responsibility: 'Only God can do it. You can do nothing.

Striving is a waste of spiritual energy. If you are not purely motivated you are wasting your time.'

The trouble with these nuggets of nonsense is that they contain just enough truth to distract us from common sense. Not my common sense, you understand—I'm talking about the common sense of Jesus. Read the parable of the two sons in Matthew 21:28–32. Read, too, what Jesus says in chapter 7, verse 21. Read about Gethsemane. Do what you're told. Sometimes it will hurt, but God will be pleased.

Prayer

Thank you for loving us, Lord. We offer you our obedience.

AP

Punishment for disobedience

But if you will not listen to me and carry out all these commands, and if you reject my decrees and abhor my laws and fail to carry out all my commands and so violate my covenant, then I will do this to you: I will bring on you sudden terror, wasting diseases and fever that will destroy your sight and sap your strength. You will plant seed in vain, because your enemies will eat it. I will set my face against you so that you will be defeated by your enemies; those who hate you will rule over you, and you will flee even when no one is pursuing you.

Have you ever deliberately disobeyed God? I have, lots of times. For instance, there was a time when I believed that I was being called to go and perform a particular, long-term task. I didn't go—simple as that. I didn't want to. It frightened me and, anyway, I wanted to do something else. I don't recall any wasting diseases or fever that destroyed my sight occurring or any sense of my enemies ruling over me as a result of this disobedience, but there certainly was a consequence. My punishment, if you want to call it that, was the kind of punishment that is a potential part of any relationship that really means something.

I was upset. It was the kind of upsetness that picks at your peace, gnaws at your ability to relax, defies your attempts at distraction. It happens in human relationships as well. You make a decision that is bound to hurt a person who loves you and, however much you try to rationalize it, you know there will be no peace until repairs have been made.

For Christians, this is the joy of love and the peril of freedom. As time goes by, we sense that the love of God is passionate and personal. He risks his own hurt by giving us freedom to make choices—and it is a real freedom. We can be disobedient if we wish, but that decision will contain within itself the risk of both suffering and causing pain. I thank God that a million new beginnings are available, but I don't want to take advantage of this freedom. I shall try to be obedient.

Prayer
I'm so sorry, Lord. Thank you.

AP

Jesus on the road: Mark 6—10

Ours must be the first generation of Christians who think pilgrimage is all about arriving rather than travelling. The destination might be the same—a place hallowed by prayer and associated with some revelation of God—but getting there in days gone by was not so easy. In the past, going on pilgrimage meant embarking on a long and often arduous journey. Nowadays, it usually means a coach trip—the greatest hardship being not much more than a traffic jam on the M25. In the past, because it involved travelling, most of the benefits of a pilgrimage were found not at the destination but on the road getting there. When you arrived, you were just as likely to be giving thanks for what you had already received as you were to be expecting to receive more.

These chapters in Mark's Gospel are about a journey. Jesus travels around Jerusalem, taking his disciples with him and they learn from him as they travel along. Jesus himself is challenged and changed by his encounters. The same can happen to us as we read these stories and reflect on our own pilgrimage with Jesus.

It is a funny, roundabout journey, though. The way is never quite as we expect. Just as we seem to be getting somewhere, Jesus challenges us to strike out in a new direction.

Several commentaries on Mark's Gospel point out that, if you were to trace the journeys made by Jesus in these chapters on a map, it would be a very strange route indeed. He appears to crisscross back and forth across the territory with little purpose or preconceived plan, but perhaps that is the point. Like those Celtic saints who got into their coracles and set off just seeing where the wind would blow them, Jesus simply gets up and starts travelling. He is going nowhere and everywhere. Every person and the whole world is his destination, but, eventually, as he circles around Palestine, his sights centre on Jerusalem. The passages we are exploring end in Jericho, but Jesus is on his way to a destiny somewhere else.

We begin in Nazareth, Jesus' home town, but he is not accepted there. Astonished by their lack of belief, Jesus takes to the road. He ends up on the outskirts of Jerusalem, ready to enter the home of his people, ready to face further rejection, ready to discover his true home, which is with God but will be found on a cross.

Stephen Cottrell

Sunday 16 August

MARK 6:1–6 (NRSV)

Leaving home

[Jesus] left that place and came to his home town, and his disciples followed him. On the sabbath he began to teach in the synagogue, and many who heard him were astounded. They said, 'Where did this man get all this? What is this wisdom that has been given to him? What deeds of power are being done by his hands! Is not this the carpenter, the son of Mary and brother of James and Joses and Judas and Simon, and are not his sisters here with us?' And they took offence at him. Then Jesus said to them, 'Prophets are not without honour, except in their home town, and among their own kin, and in their own house.' And he could do no deed of power there, except that he laid his hands on a few sick people and cured them. And he was amazed at their unbelief.

Our journey begins with one of the saddest stories in the New Testament. Jesus returns to the place where he has been brought up and where people know him best. They are astounded by his words—'Where did he get all this?' they say to each other—but they are also scornful: 'Isn't this the carpenter's boy? Pay him no heed!' Such mockery must have really hurt, especially as it follows from what seems to be a genuine appreciation that he has something worth saying. As Jesus himself concludes, however, being accepted by those who know you best is often the hardest thing of all. He is amazed by their lack of belief and he can do little for them—they have cut themselves off.

So Jesus takes to the road. It is an experience many of us know. Something happens in life—perhaps similar experiences of misunderstanding or even rejection —and we move on from what has been home to discover what will become home. This is the journey Jesus makes in these chapters. He travels through towns and villages. He gathers people around him. He teaches, admonishes, heals and provides; and we walk with him, following in his way, asking him to reach into our unbelief and heal us. We seek the gift of faith as we accompany him on the road.

Prayer

Jesus, let us walk at your side and learn how to travel through life.

SC

Sent out to share the news

Then he went about among the villages teaching. He called the twelve and began to send them out two by two, and gave them authority over the unclean spirits. He ordered them to take nothing for their journey except a staff; no bread, no bag, no money in their belts; but to wear sandals and not to put on two tunics. He said to them, 'Wherever you enter a house, stay there until you leave the place. If any place will not welcome you and they refuse to hear you, as you leave, shake off the dust that is on your feet as a testimony against them.' So they went out and proclaimed that all should repent.

So the travelling begins, but not in the way you might expect. The beginning of the journey anticipates the end. Jesus, the one who has been sent by God, the traveller on the road, sends others to journey, too, and he only asks them to take one thing with them, apart from their staff. It is not bread, bag or money, but simply their presence. This is the way that others will discover the way of the kingdom—by the presence of those who have walked with Jesus and been sent out by him.

This is why every follower of Jesus is a disciple, a follower and an apostle—one who is sent out. We are the ones who have been called to journey with Jesus (he is the one who will teach and feed us). We are the ones who have been sent out by him, to take those same provisions of wisdom and grace to the hungry and hopeless of the world.

So that is what the disciples do. Two by two, they go into the world to share God's presence. Where they find welcome, they stay. Where there is no welcome, they move on. 'Turn again' were the words on their lips, discover a new direction for life. This is what the word 'repent' really means—re-orientate. As you walk with Jesus and find yourself sent out by him, so you find another way through life.

Prayer

Wayfaring God, help me to travel faithfully with Jesus and go where he leads me. Help me to hear his call to be sent out.

SC

MARK 6:30–34 (NRSV)

The heart of the matter

The apostles gathered around Jesus, and told him all that they had done and taught. He said to them, 'Come away to a deserted place all by yourselves and rest a while.' For many were coming and going, and they had no leisure even to eat. And they went away in the boat to a deserted place by themselves. Now many saw them going and recognized them, and they hurried there on foot from all the towns and arrived ahead of them. As he went ashore, he saw a great crowd; and he had compassion for them, because they were like sheep without a shepherd; and he began to teach them many things.

The road we travel with Jesus always leads to the heart. Sometimes it is to the heart of conflict—we will encounter demons on this journey. Sometimes it is to the heart of pain—we will encounter illness and hunger. Wherever else it goes, it always leads in the end to the heart of God.

Jesus' own travels are marked by times away from the crowds and away from the competing agendas of other people's expectations. Spending time alone with God, Jesus always returns to what is his true home, where he receives comfort and affirmation. This is the place where his compass is set.

So, when the Twelve return, Jesus takes them with him to this place of rest, takes them to the heart of God. He also wants to hear about their adventures. By recounting what has happened he knows that they will understand it

more, for all good teaching begins with good listening. It is itself a healing and an affirmation. It provides a mirror in which we can see our experience clearly. God himself holds the mirror up to Jesus and, in turn, Jesus holds it for all who respond to his invitation.

Even as this rest is being prepared, however, the pressures do not let up. The crowds see where Jesus is heading and they rush around the shore ahead of him and throng around him. 'They are,' says Mark, 'like sheep without a shepherd.' In other words, they need the guidance and protection that Jesus gives to all who travel with him.

Prayer
Steadfast God, lead me to your place of rest and let me know the affirmation of your love.

SC

Feeding the hungry

He ordered [the disciples] to get all the people to sit down in groups on the green grass. So they sat down in groups of hundreds and of fifties. Taking the five loaves and the two fish, he looked up to heaven, and blessed and broke the loaves, and gave them to his disciples to set before the people; and he divided the two fish among them all. And all ate and were filled; and they took up twelve baskets full of broken pieces and of the fish. Those who had eaten the loaves numbered five thousand men.

It is getting late and the crowds are restless and hungry. As usual, the disciples get it wrong. They want to send everyone away—everyone, that is, except themselves—but Jesus wants to do the opposite. He wants to invite them all to dinner, so he tells the disciples to get them some food.

This astonishing story of God's hospitality, abundance and provision holds many layers of meaning. First, it shows Jesus' compassion. The people are hungry, so he wants to feed them. He is concerned for this most basic of their needs. He never overlooks our physicality, never spiritualizes our dis-ease.

At the same time, this is also a story about what Jesus can do with what he is offered. The disciples have no money to buy food and are truculent and despairing, yet Jesus is able to transform the few loaves and fish that they do have into a banquet for everyone.

People who are on a journey need to be fed; Jesus understands that. Therefore, it can be no coincidence that Mark writes this story in a way that reminds us of the Eucharist, which gives us supplies for our journey. It is around the Lord's table set on earth that Jesus gives us his bread, in preparation for the day when we will sit down with him at his table in the coming kingdom. The feeding of the multitudes is a sign of that which is to come, of the new creation where all are fed and transformed. And that new creation is still anticipated here and now when we hold out empty hands at Communion to receive our rations.

Prayer

Generous God, feed me with the bread of life and point my heart towards your kingdom.

SC

Blown off course

When evening came, the boat was out on the lake, and he was alone on the land. When he saw that [the disciples] were straining at the oars against an adverse wind, he came towards them early in the morning, walking on the lake. He intended to pass them by. But when they saw him walking on the lake, they thought it was a ghost and cried out; for they all saw him and were terrified. But immediately he spoke to them and said, 'Take heart, it is I; do not be afraid.' Then he got into the boat with them and the wind ceased. And they were utterly astounded, for they did not understand about the loaves, but their hearts were hardened.

Now, three different journeys begin. Jesus heads up into the mountain on his own to pray—he needs and craves the company of God. The crowds are dismissed, but they still have decisions to make about which way to go and their means to travel. The disciples go ahead of Jesus to Bethsaida, but, out on the lake, they are overcome by a fierce storm. They strain anxiously against the winds that seem set to confound them.

Early in the morning, Jesus comes towards them, walking on the lake. Then there is a strange statement: 'He intended to pass them by.' What can this mean? That he has more to show them? That he is always moving beyond them? That his agenda will always stretch and transform them? Whatever the case, when they see him they cry out, not for help, but because they are terrified: they think it is a ghost. This is when Jesus turns, towards their fear. He strengthens their resolve as he joins them in the boat and the wind dies down. He puts them back on course.

Stranger still, why are they so frightened and why are they struggling? Because they don't understand what happened with the loaves. They have not yet caught up with the transforming message of Jesus. They still think the change of direction he wants the people to take is for a chosen few alone.

Prayer

Comforting God, when I am struggling against strong winds, when I am filled with fear, when I put limits on your love, speak to my heart, draw me to yourself and put me back on track.

SC

Outside the comfort zone

From there he set out and went away to the region of Tyre... A woman whose little daughter had an unclean spirit immediately heard about him, and she came and bowed down at his feet. Now the woman was a Gentile, of Syrophoenician origin. She begged him to cast the demon out of her daughter. He said to her, 'Let the children be fed first, for it is not fair to take the children's food and throw it to the dogs.' But she answered him, 'Sir, even the dogs under the table eat the children's crumbs.' Then he said to her, 'For saying that, you may go—the demon has left your daughter.' So she went home, found the child lying on the bed, and the demon gone.

If you travel to unexpected places, you will meet unexpected people. Jesus is on the edge of Gentile territory, further north than Galilee and into Phoenicia. There he encounters a woman of guts and guile. She begs him to heal her daughter but, with what seems to be astonishing rudeness, Jesus turns her away, saying, 'It is not fair to take the children's bread and throw it to the dogs.' The inference is clear: the people of Israel are the children, she and her daughter the dogs. After all, that is how the world looked to most Jews at the time. They were the chosen people of God; everyone else was defiled and unclean.

Travel changes you, however. The woman's reply is devastating: 'Sir, even the dogs under the table eat the children's crumbs.' These words seem to expand Jesus' own understanding of his ministry, for he is to be the light and guide for *all* the world, not just Israel. If vocation is the gradual unfolding of purpose, then why shouldn't this be the case for Jesus as well, discovering as he goes along God's direction for his life, the slow refining of vocation?

It also means that we are more likely to find our vocation and the purposes of God for our lives when we move outside our comfort zones, cross boundaries, sit down with strangers, open ourselves to the unexpected. To travel is to expand your horizons.

Prayer

God, change me. Help me to cross boundaries. Expand my horizons.

SC

MARK 7:31–36 (NRSV)

The trouble with miracles

Then he returned from the region of Tyre, and went by way of Sidon towards the Sea of Galilee, in the region of the Decapolis. They brought to him a deaf man who had an impediment in his speech; and they begged him to lay his hand on him. He took him aside in private, away from the crowd, and put his fingers into his ears, and he spat and touched his tongue. Then looking up to heaven, he sighed and said to him, 'Ephphatha', that is, 'Be opened.' And immediately his ears were opened, his tongue was released, and he spoke plainly. Then Jesus ordered them to tell no one; but the more he ordered them, the more zealously they proclaimed it.

Now here's a funny thing. The more Jesus tells them to be quiet, the more they talk. Knowing human nature as he did, perhaps he reckoned that the best way to get a message out was to tell people to keep it secret. Then they were bound to blab! Alternatively, is it that news like this—a deaf man is healed—will always spread or is it something else?

Throughout Mark's Gospel, Jesus exhorts people to keep quiet about what is happening. Perhaps he worries that they will pounce on the miraculous and want more of it, but never actually join him on the road. That is the danger with the miracles—if you'll forgive me for putting it that way. The risk is that they will turn Jesus into a miracle worker and nothing else. As the story in the first chapter of these readings made clear, however, when he comes to his home town and he is not accepted, he can do very little.

Jesus is not a magician. His miracles always point beyond themselves to the promises and plenty of God's kingdom and, therefore, he always points beyond himself to God. As he goes along, he teases and provokes. Don't settle for the teaching without the teacher; for the miracles but not the God they point to. Jesus is recruiting fellow travellers, not fans.

What is the real secret? Well, it will soon unfold. Jesus is the Messiah of God, but not in the form that people expected.

Prayer

Compassionate God, help me to my feet, heal me and help me walk in your way.

SC

MARK 8:22–26 (NRSV)

Gradual revelation

They came to Bethsaida. Some people brought a blind man to him and begged him to touch him. He took the blind man by the hand and led him out of the village; and when he had put saliva on his eyes and laid his hands on him, he asked him, 'Can you see anything?' And the man looked up and said, 'I can see people, but they look like trees, walking.' Then Jesus laid his hands on his eyes again; and he looked intently and his sight was restored, and he saw everything clearly. Then he sent him away to his home, saying, 'Do not even go into the village.'

Back on home territory, another person in need is brought to Jesus. This healing story is particularly interesting because it takes Jesus two attempts to heal him. After Jesus lays hands on him the first time, the man can see, but not very clearly—his vision is sill blurred. He can see the people around him, but only as vague shapes: they look like trees, he says. So Jesus tries again and this time the man is healed.

What is even more interesting is the position that Mark gives this story in his Gospel. At this point it is worth remembering that, when Mark wrote his Gospel, he had, in all probability, collected together a large number of stories about Jesus. He puts them together to form a narrative that will illustrate his central point—that Jesus is the Messiah, the Son of God (see 1:1)

What he shows here is how recognition of this truth comes gradually. We have already noted Jesus' concern that people might be beguiled by the miraculous but stop short of actually embracing who he is, and he is concerned about this for his disciples as much as anyone else. They are with him on the road, but they have very little understanding of who he is. By placing this story of sight restored gradually here, Mark is perhaps suggesting that, just as it took this man a little while to see fully, so it will be with the disciples and, perhaps, with all who follow Jesus. We won't get it straight away, he is saying, it takes time—time on the road with Jesus—to see clearly.

Prayer

Open my eyes, Lord. Help me to see.

SC

The big question

Jesus went on with his disciples to the villages of Caesarea Philippi; and on the way he asked his disciples, 'Who do people say that I am?' And they answered him, 'John the Baptist; and others, Elijah; and still others, one of the prophets.' He asked them, 'But who do you say that I am?' Peter answered him, 'You are the Messiah.' And he sternly ordered them not to tell anyone about him.

Now comes the big one, the question that every person must face in any relationship. Who exactly is this person?

For Mark, this story of recognition is pivotal in the whole arrangement of his Gospel. From this point onwards, Jesus turns towards Jerusalem and his destiny as a Messiah who must suffer and die. First of all, though, he must find out who's with him. Who else will travel this road that he must take? So, he asks the fateful question: 'Who do people say that I am?'

The answers are predictable. 'It seems as if you are one of the prophets,' say the disciples, 'like John the Baptist or Elijah.' It is as if we asked the question today and found people saying that Jesus is a great leader, like Nelson Mandela, or a great champion for justice, like Bob Geldof.

Here, however, Jesus is not talking to bystanders who have simply observed him from a distance, those who have liked his teaching or been impressed by his signs but don't really know him. He is talking with those who have travelled with him for a long while. He wants to know what they think. 'Who do you say that I am?' he asks them. It is Peter who makes the breakthrough. It is like a light switching on in his head. 'Of course! You are the Messiah. You are the one towards whom our scriptures have been pointing; the person our nation is waiting for.'

From this point on, Peter is recruited to make a different journey. No longer is he following a great teacher; he is following God come down to earth. This journey is going to become tougher.

Prayer

Lord, help me to recognize Jesus.
Help me to see him for who he is.
Help me to follow him, especially
when the road gets rough.

SC

Expectations reversed

Then he began to teach them that the Son of Man must undergo great suffering, and be rejected by the elders, the chief priests, and the scribes, and be killed, and after three days rise again. He said all this quite openly. And Peter took him aside and began to rebuke him. But turning and looking at his disciples, he rebuked Peter and said, 'Get behind me, Satan! For you are setting your mind not on divine things but on human things.'

As soon as the recognition is made, Jesus leads his disciples on another journey. This time, though, it cannot be made on foot or by road: it is a journey into the heart. Jesus starts to teach them what being the Messiah means.

Up until this point, their expectation would have been that the Messiah would come as a conquering hero, like King David, and establish a new and independent kingdom. Jesus, however, starts to explain that it will not be like that. He is the one who is going to demonstrate God's love for all people, and he is going to do that by becoming the slaughtered and innocent lamb that was promised to Abraham when he was spared having to kill his own son, the lamb that was imagined by the prophet Isaiah when he spoke of one who would be led like a lamb to the slaughter.

We should note that, after all the talk about keeping things secret, Mark tells us that, on this subject, Jesus 'spoke quite openly'. That is because this is the heart of his message, the disclosure of the heart of God—that God aches with suffering love for all people and is going to walk the second mile of love by demonstrating his care for the world and by becoming obedient to death, even death on a cross.

This is too much for Peter. Even as he sees who Jesus is, he recoils from him. He shouts at Jesus. He complains that this cannot be right—it upsets all his notions about God and about God's kingdom. So, Jesus rebukes him: 'Get behind me, Satan.'

Prayer

Persistent God, open my heart to understand the mysteries and the depths of your love as revealed in the cross of Christ. Help me when I get things wrong.

SC

Bearing the cross

He called the crowd with his disciples, and said to them, 'If any want to become my followers, let them deny themselves and take up their cross and follow me. For those who want to save their life will lose it, and those who lose their life for my sake, and for the sake of the gospel, will save it. For what will it profit them to gain the whole world and forfeit their life? Indeed, what can they give in return for their life? Those who are ashamed of me and of my words... of them the Son of Man will also be ashamed when he comes in the glory of his Father with the holy angels.'

Now, as on so many journeys, we come to a crossroads: a decision about which direction to go in and, in this case, about something to be picked up and carried. This decision will shape every other. Jesus tells those listening that, if they want to be his followers, they must deny themselves, take up their cross and follow him.

The disciples can't have known what these words meant at that time. Even Jesus can't have been fully aware of what he was saying, but now, reading them in the light of where we know his journey ended, we see their terrible beauty. They tell us that walking with Jesus means walking the path of suffering love, sharing in his concern for the world, going the extra distance that love demands. The world may offer all sorts of riches and rewards, but they will pass away. What Jesus offers is life everlasting.

This carrying of the cross will, for all time, be the true mark of those who walk with Jesus. It is the sign that we are baptized into his dying and rising; it is our brand. What looks to the world like folly and madness is the deepest wisdom of God, revealed in the suffering and gentleness of Christ. When the world does its worst, God does his best.

Jesus is not just speaking to the disciples at this point. He is also addressing the crowd; he is addressing us.

Prayer

Jesus, give me strength to carry your cross and show your love to the world. Reveal your strength through my weakness, your wisdom through my folly and your peace through my busy, confused life.

SC

Glimpsing the future

Six days later, Jesus took with him Peter and James and John, and led them up a high mountain apart, by themselves. And he was transfigured before them, and his clothes became dazzling white, such as no one on earth could bleach them. And there appeared to them Elijah with Moses, who were talking with Jesus... Then a cloud overshadowed them, and from the cloud there came a voice, 'This is my Son, the Beloved; listen to him!'

This journey with Jesus leads from the heart to the heights. Now that his disciples are slowly realizing who he is, he takes a select few away to the top of a mountain and, in their sight, he is transfigured. It is hard to know exactly what this means, but we are told that Jesus appears to them as dazzling brightness.

There is a pattern in the Christian life of glimpsing the end in the middle. This story seems to be about the resurrection—the disciples see Jesus in a new way. He is still human, yet radiant with a light that seems to set him apart. Here, what God is going to do in Jesus in the future breaks into the present. In fact, this vision of Christ as he will become is so astonishing and so beautiful that they want to stay with it. Peter even suggests that they build some tents (vv. 5–6). Poor Peter—he always gets it wrong! The vision is given to sustain them in what lies ahead, although it does not prevent them from fleeing when things get really difficult. They have to go back down the mountain, return to the road. A voice from heaven directs them: 'This is my Son... listen to him!

This voice from God can direct us, too. If we want to know how to navigate through life, we must listen to Jesus. He shows us where to go and, in him, we glimpse our destination: a new creation, where the stuff of this world, and of human life, is gathered up by God and recreated. We are not meant to stay where we have had disclosures of who God is, but move on, carrying them with us.

Prayer

God, show me who you are. Direct the journey of my life. Sustain me when the going is hard.

SC

Greatest and least

Then they came to Capernaum; and when he was in the house he asked them, 'What were you arguing about on the way?' But they were silent, for on the way they had argued with one another about who was the greatest. He sat down, called the twelve, and said to them, 'Whoever wants to be first must be last of all and servant of all.' Then he took a little child and put it among them; and taking it in his arms, he said to them, 'Whoever welcomes one such child in my name welcomes me, and whoever welcomes me welcomes not me but the one who sent me.'

Here is some sobering news for all those seasoned travellers who think that they might be getting somewhere. A little child is out there ahead of you! The disciples have been arguing with each other about which of them is the greatest. Vanity and ambition rule their lives. You know the situation: the office bore, the pushy parent, the jovial drunk. They all have one thing in common—they love to tell you how brilliant, how well qualified, well connected, experienced, well educated, charming and influential they are.

Jesus must either be bored rigid or spitting mad. Either way, he pulls the carpet out from under their complacent feet by leading a little child out of the crowd and telling them that this is the person who is first in the kingdom of God. Why? Because greatness in the kingdom is not measured by achievements—although this does not let us off the hook in terms of doing all we can to build God's kingdom in the world. Kingdom greatness is measured by our readiness to serve, by the ways in which we are open to receive. Indeed, Jesus says later on that it is only by becoming like little children that we can enter the kingdom at all (10:15).

Jesus goes even further. When we receive a child, when we offer service to those on the edge, those without power or influence, then we are receiving him.

Prayer

Lord, save me from the pride that makes me feel better than others, makes me imagine I am further down the road than them. Give me a servant heart, one that is tuned to the values of your kingdom.

SC

Giving it all up

As he was setting out on a journey, a man ran up and knelt before him, and asked him, 'Good Teacher, what must I do to inherit eternal life?' Jesus said to him, 'Why do you call me good? No one is good but God alone. You know the commandments: "You shall not murder; You shall not commit adultery; You shall not steal; You shall not bear false witness; You shall not defraud; Honour your father and mother."' He said to him, 'Teacher, I have kept all these since my youth.' Jesus, looking at him, loved him and said, 'You lack one thing; go, sell what you own, and give the money to the poor, and you will have treasure in heaven; then come, follow me.' When he heard this, he was shocked and went away grieving, for he had many possessions.

Another turn in the road and this time Jesus encounters a wealthy young man who is eager to know God and who faithfully declares that he has done all he can to live by God's commandments. There is still one thing he lacks, however—Jesus tells him to sell his belongings, give the money to the poor and then join him on the road. The man is shocked by this challenge. He walks away downhearted. He cannot do it. The reason? He has many possessions.

Now Jesus doesn't ask all of us to give up everything in order to follow him, but he does ask us to look at what we carry and see it differently. Many of us are possessed by our possessions. They stop us living the way that we should. They force us to look at each other with fear. They distort the way we view the world and trick us into thinking that happiness can be found by consuming. Retail therapy is actually retail addiction and a road to nowhere.

Take heart. This passage also contains one of the loveliest sentences in the Bible, in verse 21: 'Jesus, looking at him, loved him.' Jesus looked at him and loved him even as he failed to do what Jesus asked. He carried on looking at him and loving him even as he walked away, just as he carries on looking at and loving us, whether we follow him or not.

Prayer
*Loving God, set me free
to travel light.*

SC

The roads converge

They were on the road, going up to Jerusalem, and Jesus was walking ahead of them; they were amazed, and those who followed were afraid. He took the twelve aside again and began to tell them what was to happen to him, saying, 'See, we are going up to Jerusalem, and the Son of Man will be handed over to the chief priests and the scribes, and they will condemn him to death; then they will hand him over to the Gentiles; they will mock him, and spit upon him, and flog him, and kill him; and after three days he will rise again.'

Again, Jesus warns his disciples that he must suffer. Again, they fail to understand. If you read on from this passage, you will find them arguing with each other once more, wanting places at his right hand in glory, failing to see how this glory is going to be revealed.

The road is now bringing them closer to Jerusalem. The city is on the horizon. All the roads Jesus has travelled now converge into this one. He knows that this city is where his journey on earth must end, where he will lay down the burdens that he carries. This is his destination, the place where the forces of sin and death will do their worst. Their aim is always to contort and misdirect. They are like a force field that interferes with the natural compass of life, but Jesus will destroy them. He will establish a stronger field of love and all who walk towards him will be safe and well, the direction of their life will be clear.

In this moment, however, the final confrontation with evil is still ahead of him and those to whom he looks for comfort seem as dim-witted and uncomprehending as ever. Can we imagine how this might have felt for Jesus, to be so misunderstood? How does it feel for him today? How must he feel when we, his Church, still get so much wrong, carrying on with our squabbles about power and position, arguing with each other and failing to show the lost and rootless of the world the way that leads to life?

Prayer

Lord, help us to see the meaning of the cross—its beauty and is power. Help us to walk towards it and be directed by its light.

SC

Lord, have mercy

They came to Jericho. As he and his disciples and a large crowd were leaving Jericho, Bartimaeus son of Timaeus, a blind beggar, was sitting by the roadside. When he heard that it was Jesus of Nazareth, he began to shout out and say, 'Jesus, Son of David, have mercy on me!' Many sternly ordered him to be quiet, but he cried out even more loudly, 'Son of David, have mercy on me!' Jesus stood still and said, 'Call him here.' And they called the blind man, saying to him, 'Take heart; get up, he is calling you.' So throwing off his cloak, he sprang up and came to Jesus. Then Jesus said to him, 'What do you want me to do for you?' The blind man said to him, 'My teacher, let me see again.' Jesus said to him, 'Go; your faith has made you well.' Immediately he regained his sight and followed him on the way.

'What do you want me to do for you?' says Jesus. What beautiful words! It took Jesus two attempts to heal the blind man we met on the road earlier, but, by contrast, this man is healed at once. By placing this story here, it is as if Mark is showing us the clarity of Jesus' purpose. Approaching the outskirts of Jerusalem, the way ahead is painfully clear and Jesus is bold in what he offers: service to those in need, clarity of vision to those who have lost their sight.

In the events that follow, most of Jesus' disciples abandon him, but to all those who cry out, 'Son of David, have mercy on me', he will respond. However much the world tells us to be quiet, insisting that this Jesus is not much more than a beguiling teacher from a long gone age, he will answer us. He will stand before us and ask us what we want. Although there are many things that we may imagine we would ask for, surely there is nothing better than this—to see God, know who he is and see his purpose for our lives. All this is given to us when we join Jesus on the road.

Prayer

Jesus, Son of God, born of Mary, have mercy on us. Renew our faith, help us to see and believe.

SC

The BRF
Magazine

Richard Fisher writes...

For many charities, income from legacies is crucial and represents a significant aspect of their funding each year. Legacies enable charities to plan ahead and provide the funding to develop new projects. Legacies make a significant difference to the ability of charities to achieve their purpose.

In this way, a legacy to support our *Barnabas* children's ministry can make a huge difference. Five years ago, we received one legacy gift that covered over half of the costs for the team for a whole year. This provided the vital funding that we needed to develop *Barnabas* in those early years.

'If you plan for a decade, plant trees; if you plan for a century, plant children' (origin unknown). Many of BRF's readers were introduced to the Bible and the Christian faith as children. Today, in both primary schools and churches, our *Barnabas* team is carrying on that same ministry of enabling children under 11, and the adults who work with them, to explore Christianity creatively.

A gift to BRF in your will can give lasting support to our work. All of our ministry needs to be planned on a long-term basis if it's to achieve maximum effectiveness, and your legacy gift will help to make this possible. For example, it could enable us to develop and pilot a new theme to offer as part of

our *Barnabas* RE Day creative arts programme. And there is a host of new *Barnabas* projects and initiatives that we would love to be able to develop if we could just secure the funding necessary.

Your legacy gift would be a huge support to our vital ministry and would help us to introduce successive generations of children to the Bible and the Christian faith. BRF has been helping people of all ages to experience the living God and to grow as disciples of Jesus Christ through the Bible, prayer and worship for over 85 years.

Today, fewer children are growing up with any real knowledge or understanding of the Bible or Christian teaching. Through our *Barnabas* children's ministry in schools and churches, we are trying to do something about this. With your help and support we can make a difference.

If you would like to discuss how your legacy gift could support a particular aspect of our *Barnabas* ministry please write to me at BRF.

BRF in Barbados

Karen Laister

In May 2008, I had the enormous privilege of travelling to Barbados to visit Madeleine Smith, our BRF Group Secretary for the island, who was retiring after having held the role for the last two decades. I was glad to be able to thank her on behalf of all of us at BRF for the work she has done in distributing our Bible reading notes to the parishes in Barbados.

We are very grateful to Madeleine for the way in which she has undertaken this task. For Madeleine, it has been her Christian ministry and vocation in her later years.

In 1995, BRF launched the *Barnabas* imprint. During the last few years, *Barnabas* has grown: it is no longer just a publishing imprint but a ministry that reflects our face-to-face work in churches and schools within the UK. The apostle Barnabas was given that name because it means 'the encourager', and I believe that Madeleine was the encourager for both the people of Barbados and for BRF.

Madeleine undertook the task of distributing the BRF notes because she had a vision. BRF itself was born out of a vision, when Canon Mannering

Bible reading and prayer form an important part of the Christian life

started writing Bible reading notes in 1922 for members of his congregation in a church in south London. It grew because those Bible reading notes met a need, and it soon spread throughout the UK and then to Anglican churches around the world.

Regular Bible reading and prayer form an important part of the Christian life. Without this regular discipline, we cannot know God. Madeleine recognized and knew for herself just how central daily prayer and Bible reading are for a healthy Christian life. Because they had made such a difference to her own life, she wanted to share them with others so they too could root their lives in Jesus Christ and his word.

Her desire is to see others grow in their understanding of God and of what he has to say to us through his word. She longs to see Christians become mature in their faith and to be challenged. When we pray and read the Bible, it changes us. It brings us comfort, joy and help in times of trouble, but it also challenges our faith. It gives us the capacity to cope when life is tough and it teaches us about God's plan for his people and his kingdom. In deepening our understanding about the Bible, we discover a God who longs to reach out and touch people. Our faith should never be a private or personal thing but something that makes us open to share the hope that is within us and able to talk about the salvation we have in Christ.

Madeleine had this ministry of encouragement among the parishes of Barbados

Christian discipleship is about helping others live out their Christian faith in all fullness. Meeting together Sunday by Sunday is vital and Bible reading notes supplement the worship and teaching we receive each week. Madeleine recognized that the Christian faith is not just for Sunday but that we need to be equipped to live out our Christian lives in the home, in school and at work.

In 1 Thessalonians 5:11 Paul tells us, 'Therefore encourage one another and build each other up, just as in fact you are doing' (NIV). Madeleine had this ministry of encouragement among the parishes of Barbados. She encouraged them so that they might be better equipped to serve God, his church and one another.

Another role that Madeleine exercised in her ministry was that of a servant. She has been a faithful distributor of the Bible reading notes. She has been involved in unpacking and counting and ensuring that the notes get to the different parishes on the island. She has also had the frustrating tasks of dealing with money, brokers, customs and long-distance communication with BRF's office in England. She has done this willingly and seen it as part of the process of getting the Bible reading notes to God's people.

We can learn, too, from this servant ministry. Madeleine recognized what God had been calling her to do; she had a clear vision for it and she quietly got on with the less-than-glamorous bits of it.

What confirms Madeleine's vision and ministry, for me, is the care she took in thinking about who should do the job next. She quietly prayed and waited for the right person to come along to take on the task. Can't waiting be hard? But also, isn't this the pattern in which the early Church operated at times? It prayed and waited. I sense that, for Madeleine, behind some of that waiting was the knowledge that God wanted to continue and grow this ministry.

Madeleine is also supported by Canon Winston Layne and St James' Church, who allowed the ministry of BRF to be based there.

BRF has changed a great deal in the last decade and since I last visited Barbados. Our ministry has diversified. At the heart of any ministry are people and relationships. The relationships and the BRF family on Barbados are something we value. We give thanks for them, their support and prayers for us.

As Madeleine steps down from an active role of distributing the notes and hands the baton to Jean Chamberlain during the course of 2008, I know that Jean and Angela, who is helping her, will receive the same support from the church family in Barbados as Madeleine did. In talking with Jean, I was so pleased to see that she was already very familiar with BRF's wider ministry, including the Bible reading notes, books and resources for children's workers.

It is good to take time to reflect and acknowledge a person's ministry within the church. Madeleine has done an amazing job and it is right that we should stop and give thanks for her and her ministry among us. Madeleine, thank you for your partnership in the gospel, your passion to see lives transformed through Bible reading and prayer, and for your living faith which is a shining example to us all.

Madeleine, thank you for your partnership in the gospel

Being a Group Secretary is not a glamorous job, but is much needed nonetheless. At BRF we are aware of the hard work put in by all our representatives around the UK and further afield, in collecting payments, keeping track of group members and promoting Bible reading in their churches. It is a job that perhaps is overlooked but, without it, things would be considerably more chaotic. We would like to thank all of you who look after BRF Groups and work tirelessly to supply Bible reading notes in your local area. It is you and your ministry within the church that helps bring the word of God to more people every day.

Karen Laister is General Manager of BRF, responsible for telling the world about BRF books and Bible reading notes and ensuring the customer services and office facilities run smoothly.

Foundations21: a fresh approach for churches

Ceri Ellis

It's often said that discipleship is needed not just on Sunday, but every day of the week. But it can be easy to forget this from Monday to Saturday. *Foundations21* is an innovative web-based resource for discipleship that can help to enrich your Christian life, both inside and outside church. It explores twelve key building blocks of the Christian faith—including prayer, the cross and mission—in a blend of online study, group interaction and personal application.

We have launched an initiative to encourage churches to make *Foundations21* an integral part of their learning and fellowship. There are many ways in which you can use it to bring discipleship alive in your congregation. Here are just a few suggestions.

The twelve topics covered in *Foundations21* lend themselves to a through-the-year preaching series. There are also links to the material within *Foundations21* that will be relevant to the following week's lectionary readings.

Foundations21 includes a wealth of learning activities, which could be used in a cell or home group. There is a video programme and discussion questions for each of the main sections.

A small group of new Christians could be accompanied as they progress from a Christian basics course. Alternatively, you could use *Foundations21* to encourage mature Christians to start one-to-one mentoring and discipling with individuals or in small accountability groups.

For those who want to be involved in small groups but can't attend regularly because of work, travel or family commitments, *Foundations21* could provide a way of staying connected.

When your church registers free with *Foundations21*, members of your congregation can subscribe at the special church rate of £39.99 per person (normal price £59.99).

For more information on *Foundations21*, contact the BRF office on 01865 319700 and ask for the *Foundations21* Churches leaflet. Alternatively, you can visit the website: www.brf.org.uk/pages/1322s.htm.

An extract from
Bible Reading—a Beginner's Guide

This highly accessible book by Michael Green sets out straightforward and helpful strategies for those who are completely new to Bible reading. He explains how to enjoy the Bible, how to read it by ourselves and with others, and how we in turn can start to share its teaching with new Christians. The following is an abridged extract from Chapter 2, 'What can it do for me?'

'What's in it for me?' is a very natural question, particularly in today's fast-moving society, where we are too busy to bother with anything that does not have some immediate relevance. No wonder, then, that people ask that kind of question about Bible reading: 'What's the point? What can it do for me?' It can do a great deal.

Years ago there was a young French scholar called Émile Caillet, who was determined to discover truth. He… spent some ten years studying all the philosophy systems that had ever been devised. He was disappointed with what he found, so he said, 'I will write my own philosophy'—and he did. However, when he looked back over it some time later, he was again disappointed with what he had written. He despaired of ever finding truth.

One day he came home and found his wife reading the Bible. 'Get that book of superstition out of my house,' he roared. She refused. Instead, she pleaded with

him at least to glance at its contents. With a bad grace he did, and he was entirely captivated by what he read. Here was the teaching which had so long eluded him… He became a Christian. In due course his biblical studies led him to become a theologian. Indeed, he spent many fruitful years as a professor at Princeton Seminary in the USA. Looking back on the whole experience, he said, 'At last I have found a book which understands me.'

The Bible has always had this life-changing power. In the early days of the Church, a very able intellectual, Justin… had studied the Platonic, Aristotelian and Cynic philosophical systems of the ancient world and, like Caillet, he was disappointed because none of them had the ring of truth about them that he was looking for. One day he met an old man in the fields, who, seeing his philosopher's cloak, asked him what the true philosophy was. Justin was, of course, unable to give a satisfactory reply because he had not found it himself. So the old man asked him to read and reflect on a copy of the scriptures. Justin was reluctant to examine these 'barbaric writings', as he described them. But he did, and he was never the same again. He found that the scriptures 'possess a terrible power in themselves' and also 'a wonderful sweetness', which made an incredible impression on him. He became a follower of Jesus. He refused to lay aside his philosopher's cloak but fearlessly proclaimed the 'true philosophy' that he found in the scriptures throughout his life…

Charles Dickens put the matter very succinctly: 'The New Testament is the best book the world has ever known and will ever know.' 'It is more than a book to me,' reflected Napoleon, in exile on St Helena. 'It is, as it were, a person.' It has an astonishing power to address us personally, as if it were written for us alone. 'It is talking to me and about me,' said the Danish philosopher, Søren Kierkegaard. Perhaps that is why no sceptical criticism, no persecution, no confiscation, no sanctions against reading this book have ever succeeded. Its sales just go on growing: there is no other book in the same league.

But let's be specific. What can it do for you?

First and foremost, it can change your life… The written word can put you in touch with Jesus, the living Word (or self-disclosure) of God. Just as you can only know my unseen thoughts if I clothe them in words, so we can only know the unseen God if he communicates to us in words we can take in. That he has done…

Once people start reading it with an open heart, God is able to get through to them. John's Gospel embodies that claim very clearly. He tells us why he wrote his book. It was so 'that you may believe that Jesus is the Christ, the Son of God, and that by believing you may have life in his name' (John 20:31).

Notice the two stages in that purpose. The first one is calculated to show the reader what John himself discovered by personal companionship with Jesus—that he really is the Son of God. John gives us in his Gospel seven great signs that Jesus did, followed by the supreme sign of his death and resurrection. These convinced John himself, and he records them for others so that they may see solid grounds for belief. But it can never rest there. Jesus is the one who gives a new dimension to life—a spiritual rebirth, no less. That is what John wants for his readers, that they may have 'life in his name'. Had not Jesus proclaimed, 'I have come that they may have life, and have it to the full' (John 10:10)?

… Once we have discovered the new life in Christ, scripture is able to build us up and show us more and more of the treasures we have inherited as Christians (Acts 20:32). It is a gradual process. We are not dropped into the deep end all at once. While there are lots of things we shall not understand, there is plenty that we can readily take on board and find really nourishing—particularly in the Gospels and Psalms. The Bible calls itself milk, milk for babies in the Christian life… (1 Peter 2:2).

Of course, we are not meant to stay at that level for long, but to develop. Wouldn't it be disappointing if a nursing baby never got on to solid food? Accordingly, the Bible also compares itself to meat for those who are mature. Paul has reason to complain of some of the Christians at Corinth, whom he himself had led to Christ, 'I gave you milk, not solid food, for you were not yet ready for it. Indeed, you are still not ready' (1 Corinthians 3:2). Sadly, that is true of so many Christians today. They are semi-starved. They have not been built up in their spiritual lives by the scriptures…

The Bible itself contains some marvellous images of what it can do. It is like a fire, to warm our hearts when they are cold. '"Is not my word like fire," declares the Lord, "and like a hammer that breaks a rock in pieces?"' (Jeremiah 23:29). I don't know about you, but my heart is often both cold and rock-like. I need to have that rock broken up, that fire lit up. That is what scripture can do when we come to it humbly.

Here is something else. The Bible is described as the sword that the Holy Spirit uses to fight for us in times of temptation (Ephesians 6:17). The classic example of this, of course, is the use Jesus himself made of some verses he seems to have committed to memory from the book of Deuteronomy (Matthew 4:1–11). In each case, that 'sword of the Spirit' drove the tempter away. Try it. It works!

No wonder the prophet Ezekiel saw the portion of the scriptures that had been written in his day as something wonderfully sweet. 'He said to me, "… eat this scroll I am giving you and fill your stomach with it." So I ate it, and it tasted as sweet as honey in my mouth' (Ezekiel 3:3). Bizarre imagery, perhaps, but wonderfully clear teaching! The psalmist, too… found it sweet and nourishing to his soul, and so will we if only we will start reading a bit of it on a daily basis. It will build us up and be 'a lamp to our feet and a light for our path' (Psalm 119:105). We all need a bit of illumination and guidance in the problems that beset us daily, and you will be amazed to find that in your daily reading you often get just the insight and direction that you were looking for…

To order a copy of this book, please turn to the order form on page 159.

Hasta la Fiesta!

Lucy Moore

I've recently bought a new car and had to restrain myself from buying a Ford Fiesta, as so many people have sniggered reminiscently about the old 'messy Fiesta' of their student days. While *Barnabas*' Messy Fiestas have many similarities to the car—they go all over the country, they're cheerful, colourful and they bring people together—I fear it wouldn't work to push the comparison further. So if I've bought a Clio rather than a Ford, what is everyone talking about when they mention a 'Messy Fiesta'?

It's all rather exciting. Back in 2004 my own church of St Wilfrid's in Cowplain began a Fresh Expression of church for families (in the broadest sense of the word) who can't attend Sunday morning services, for whatever reason. Because it isn't just a club, we called it 'church' and because almost every aspect of it is messy it was called 'Messy Church'. It welcomed 60 people to its first monthly gathering and numbers have remained between 40 and 100 ever since. After the *Fresh Expressions* DVD came out, with a slot on Messy Church, people from all over the country started thinking that here was a pattern they could usefully follow in their outreach to families. Sometime later, Barnabas published a book, *Messy Church*, which has sold over 2500 copies, and it wasn't long before we were having contact not only with UK churches interested

in the idea, but with churches from other English-speaking countries, too.

At *Barnabas*, we realized that God was starting something potentially huge through our small messy efforts, and, with the full agreement and blessing of St Wilf's, decided that we had a responsibility to encourage and resource the leaders of these other Messy Churches in whatever way we could. One way was to start the website as a place for people to share ideas and for me to keep the wider Messy Churches in touch with any developments. www.messychurch.org.uk was launched in 2007.

But *Barnabas* has always known the value of bringing people face to face with each other to grow in their knowledge and love of God, and in this spirit we decided to run some training days across the country—meeting places for people involved with Messy Church or thinking about getting involved. They would be times of catching the bigger vision from God's word and from each other, thinking and praying creatively, swapping insights with Christians from all denominations, eating together, doing craft together, and simply chatting about a shared passion together—that of seeing people of all ages come closer to Jesus. Because we decided from the start that they were going to be fun, lively and celebratory in nature, with the emphasis on sharing and generosity, the title 'Training Days on Messy Church' didn't work at all, and the more upbeat 'Messy Fiestas' came into being.

The other aspect of Messy Fiestas that will be more and more important as the years pass is the vital necessity for developing Messy Church if it isn't going to stagnate. We need to hear and affirm the ways that different Messy Churches are hearing God's encouragement to go forward in outreach and discipleship so that we can all gain wisdom from each other's experience.

We decided to organize five Fiestas, each based near the homes of the far-flung full-time *Barnabas* team members. It was interesting to find that as soon as we made these public, there was not only interest from people wishing to attend the Fiestas, but also a flow of enquiries about whether we could come and run a Fiesta in other places too—from Truro to Norwich and, most gloriously, Chester. (Why? Well, the Cowplain Fiesta sounds good, but the Chester Fiesta rolls off the tongue with glee. I'm desperate for someone to trump it by asking for a Leicester Fiesta.)

The Messy Fiestas over 2008 have been immensely rewarding days. The energy and goodwill of the people who have attended have been incredible. The way that new ideas are already coming out of the discussions at the Fiestas justifies their whole existence. The network of people now in touch with each other and enabled to communicate with each other is growing month by month.

And we can be joyful about knowing that we're part of a network of like-minded churches across the world. Two visitors from Toronto attended the Bedford Fiesta and are keen to arrange a similar Fiesta over in Canada to inspire and encourage churches there. Steve Croft calls Messy Church 'one of the more glorious exports of Portsmouth Diocese'. How glorious indeed that a city which has always been the starting point for travellers and ideas to go round the globe should also be the starting place for God's work to shoot off round the world with all the acceleration of... well, a Ford Fiesta.

Lucy Moore is a key member of the Barnabas team, based in the South of England.

The Year of the Child

Martyn Payne

'Understand that all children are precious. Give us the things we need to make us happy and strong, and always do your best for us whenever we are in your care.' These words (taken from *For Every Child: the rights of the child in words and pictures*, Red Fox, 2002) are a summary of Article 3 from the United Nations Convention on the Rights of the Child. This year is the 30th anniversary of the publication of these Rights of the Child and, in recognition of this, 2009 has been designated 'The Year of the Child'.

Of course, we needn't just look to the United Nations Charter to be reminded of our responsibilities towards children. The Bible challenges us to pass on what is precious to the next generation (Deuteronomy 4:9) and care for the vulnerable in our midst (Psalm 10:14); Jesus' words in the Gospels about children afford them a status and an importance that the Church has often struggled to recognize: 'Jesus called a child over and made the child stand near him. Then he said: I promise you this. If you don't change and become like a child, you will never get into the kingdom of heaven' (Matthew 18:2–3, CEV). Theologians and church leaders down the centuries have hesitated over these words of Jesus. The fact that children should be models for our adult discipleship turns all conventional thinking on its head.

In the light of all this, it is exciting to realize that when BRF first began to wonder how to widen its work, it came up with the idea of developing a special strand to resource leaders who work with children. It was both innovative and inspired. Under Richard Fisher's leadership and Sue Doggett's guiding hand, *Barnabas* is now a nationally recognized team of professional trainers and consultants in children's work as well as an envied range of books and resources. The team is able to resource and equip leaders and ministers, and acts as an advocate for the inclusion of children in the life and witness of the church.

Barnabas books, web articles and ideas are now widely used and we regularly receive positive feedback and reviews for our work and the materials on offer. But BRF's investment in children is nothing more than a response to that Bible command 'to tell (these things) to the next generation' (Psalm 78:4) and, indeed, Jesus' invitation to 'let the children come to me' (Matthew 19:14.

If the story of our faith is not passed on to our children, if we neglect to provide a safe, welcoming place where children are valued, then we are in danger of becoming stumbling blocks to his little ones.

Barnabas is now an integral and lively part of all that BRF stands for, and *Barnabas* continues to grow. Our work with churches is becoming increasingly influential, particularly in the area of mentoring for children's leaders new models of church that are inclusive of children, developing positive relationships between churches and schools and resourcing faith in the home.

Recently we received this comment by email:

A really heartfelt thank you. My colleague and I have been trying to run a church children's group and the brand new all-age worship at church… and had quite simply run out of steam and inspiration… Then I found your website and we feel not only inspired but also full of new energy. Thank you so much—you are the answer to prayers!

It is a privilege to receive such feedback on our *Barnabas* work and this article is an opportunity to thank you for your prayers and support for this aspect of BRF's work, which have been so richly answered.

In this 'Year of the Child', I wonder what new initiatives your church is developing to make sure that every child in the area has an opportunity to come close to God and to be included positively in all you do as a church. Perhaps *Barnabas* can help you think this through?

After all, there is an even greater promise that Jesus makes about children, which still makes me gasp in amazement, namely that 'when you welcome even a child because of me, you welcome me' (Mark 9:37). Certainly the United Nations got it right: a world that does not pay attention to the rights of children is a world courting disaster. Even more seriously, a church that does not welcome and value children, according to this promise, is a church that cannot hope to encounter more of God and his great love.

If you would like to learn more about the spirituality of children, may I recommend two books published by Barnabas: *The Growth of Love: Understanding five essential elements of child development* by Dr Keith J. White, and *From the Ground Up: Understanding the spiritual world of the child* by Kathryn Copsey. For new ideas for your children's ministry, please visit www.barnabasinchurches.org.uk

Martyn Payne is a key member of the Barnabas team, based in London. He is the author of Footsteps to the Feast *(BRF, 2007)*

The Editor recommends

Naomi Starkey

Over recent years, BRF has continued to develop a strong range of books to help church leaders in their task of shaping the life of local congregations and encouraging mission. While at one time 'mission' meant a week of special outreach events with a visiting speaker, in the hope of recruiting new members, these days it is identified as being at the heart of what it means to be a living, healthy and growing church.

In biological terms, one of the signs of life in any organism is change—and it is interesting to reflect that the body of Christ is no different. Change, as many a harassed minister knows all too well, can be one of the hardest issues to manage. Even when outside authorities agree that change is essential for a church to survive, let alone thrive and take on a mission-focused identity, resistance from existing members (for a variety of good and bad reasons) can lead to stormy times and even complete pastoral breakdown in some difficult situations.

Phil Potter is Director of Pioneer Ministry in Liverpool diocese, involved in national strategies for promoting cell church and Fresh Expressions of church. He was previously vicar of St Mark's, Haydock, and in his 19 years there he led the church through a significant and far-reaching programme of change, with profound consequences for

Christian witness in the wider area. Having written *The Challenge of Cell Church* (BRF, 2001), he has now tackled the often vexed subject of change in a book entitled *The Challenge of Change*. The subtitle spells out its far-reaching agenda: 'A guide to shaping change and changing the shape of church'.

Decisions on what and how and when change comes about inevitably affect growth or decline in a church, and often have a major impact on people. Leaders can end up burnt out by their attempts to bring about change, or by simply facing up to the challenge of it, while congregations are left damaged and disillusioned because they could not catch the vision. What Phil Potter offers in his new book is a map for healthy and godly change.

Writing as a pastor and practitioner, he explains ways of shaping change of any kind in the life of a church and presents a guide to understanding the changing shape of church, in particular the Fresh Expressions of church now emerging. This is a book for leaders wanting to take their congregations on a journey of change, and for church members preparing to embark on a particular project or simply wanting to be equipped for whatever lies ahead. It speaks sensitively to reluctant traditionalists as well as to impatient visionaries; it has wise advice for small, struggling congregations as well as large, thriving churches. Also included are over 100 questions that can be used for personal reflection or wider group discussion.

Worship is a key facet of church life that provokes perhaps more than its fair share of conflict when any kind of change is introduced. Another new book from BRF has the somewhat provocative title *How Would Jesus Lead Worship?*—a salutary reminder that worship should be about what honours God and is in tune with a biblically based worldview, rather than simply a matter of our personal musical or liturgical preference.

The thinking behind the choice of title is straightforward: if we are trying to live as Jesus' disciples, what does it mean for us to worship as he worshipped? Authors Sam and Sara Hargreaves examine what we can learn from the life of Jesus about the foundational values for our worship. They draw on their experience as worship leaders to offer both down-to-earth teaching and many practical and creative examples, ideas and exercises to help all those involved in leading church worship.

Sam and Sara run Engage (www.engageworship.org), a new expression of the Music and Worship Foundation, which exists to resource and train all shapes and sizes of church in using a breadth of worship and musical styles. Sam also works part-time as Worship Minister at St James', Hemingford Grey, Cambridgeshire. Previously they spent five years growing the worship and creative life at a south London church, and they have also been involved in musical and creative worship at Spring Harvest, New Wine and the Baptist Assembly. The book arose partly from their studies at the London School of Theology, where they focused on the relationship between theology, music and worship.

They are particularly keen to show how worship is so much more than 'singing songs [or hymns]'. Ultimately, it is about allowing God's Holy Spirit to inspire our praise, so that it not only glorifies God but begins to transform us. As we worship, we will find taking root within our hearts Christ-like attitudes towards God, one another, our community and the wider world.

To order a copy of either of these books, please turn to the order form on page 159.

New Daylight © BRF 2009

The Bible Reading Fellowship
15 The Chambers, Vineyard, Abingdon OX14 3FE
Tel: 01865 319700; Fax: 01865 319701
E-mail: enquiries@brf.org.uk; Website: www.brf.org.uk

ISBN 978 1 84101 517 0

Distributed in Australia by:
Willow Connection, PO Box 288, Brookvale, NSW 2100.
Tel: 02 9948 3957; Fax: 02 9948 8153;
E-mail: info@willowconnection.com.au
Available also from all good Christian bookshops in Australia.
For individual and group subscriptions in Australia:
Mrs Rosemary Morrall, PO Box W35, Wanniassa, ACT 2903.

Distributed in New Zealand by:
Scripture Union Wholesale, PO Box 760, Wellington
Tel: 04 385 0421; Fax: 04 384 3990; E-mail: suwholesale@clear.net.nz

Distributed in Canada by:
The Anglican Book Centre, 80 Hayden Street, Toronto, Ontario, M4Y 3G2
Tel: 001 416 924-1332; Fax: 001 416 924-2760;
E-mail: abc@anglicanbookcentre.com; Website: www.anglicanbookcentre.com

Publications distributed to more than 60 countries

Acknowledgments
The New Revised Standard Version of the Bible, Anglicized Edition, copyright © 1989, 1995 by the
Division of Christian Education of the National Council of the Churches of Christ in the USA. Used
by permission. All rights reserved.

The Holy Bible, New International Version, copyright © 1973, 1978, 1984 by International Bible
Society. Used by permission of Hodder & Stoughton Publishers, a division of Hodder Headline Ltd.
All rights reserved. 'NIV' is a registered trademark of International Bible Society. UK trademark
number 1448790.

The Holy Bible, Today's New International Version, copyright © 2004 by International Bible Society.
Used by permission of Hodder & Stoughton Publishers, a division of Hodder Headline Ltd. All
rights reserved. 'TNIV' is a registered trademark of International Bible Society.

The Contemporary English Version, copyright © American Bible Society 1991, 1992, 1995. Used by
permission/Anglicizations copyright © British and Foreign Bible Society 1997.

New King James Version of the Bible copyright © 1979, 1980, 1982 by Thomas Nelson, Inc.
All rights reserved.

Scripture quotations from THE MESSAGE. Copyright © by Eugene H. Peterson 1993, 1994, 1995.
Used by permission of NavPress Publishing Group.

The Revised Common Lectionary is copyright © The Consultation on Common Texts, 1992 and is
reproduced with permission. *The Christian Year: Calendar, Lectionary and Collects,* which includes the
Common Worship lectionary (the Church of England's adaptations of the *Revised Common Lectionary,*
published as the Principal Service lectionary) is copyright © The Central Board of Finance of the
Church of England, 1995, 1997, and material from it is reproduced with permission.

Printed in Singapore by Craft Print International Ltd

BRF is a Christian charity committed to resourcing the spiritual journey of adults and children alike. For adults, BRF publishes Bible reading notes and books and offers an annual programme of quiet days and retreats. Under its children's imprint *Barnabas*, BRF publishes a wide range of books for those working with children under 11 in school, church and home. BRF's *Barnabas Ministry* team offers INSET sessions for primary teachers, training for children's leaders in church, quiet days, and a range of events to enable children themselves to engage with the Bible and its message.

We need your help if we are to make a real impact on the local church and community. In an increasingly secular world people need even more help with their Bible reading, their prayer and their discipleship. We can do something about this, but our resources are limited. With your help, if we all do a little, together we can make a huge difference.

How can you help?

- You could support BRF's ministry with a donation or standing order (using the response form overleaf).

- You could consider making a bequest to BRF in your will, and so give lasting support to our work. (We have a leaflet available with more information about this, which can be requested using the form overleaf.)

- And, most important of all, you could support BRF with your prayers.

Whatever you can do or give, we thank you for your support.

BRF – resourcing your spiritual journey

BRF MINISTRY APPEAL RESPONSE FORM

Name _____

Address _____

_____ Postcode _____

Telephone _____ Email _____

(tick as appropriate)

Gift Aid Declaration

☐ I am a UK taxpayer. I want BRF to treat as Gift Aid Donations all donations I make from 6 April 2000 until I notify you otherwise.

Signature _____ Date _____

☐ I would like to support BRF's ministry with a regular donation by standing order (please complete the Banker's Order below).

Standing Order – Banker's Order

To the Manager, Name of Bank/Building Society _____

Address _____

_____ Postcode _____

Sort Code _____ Account Name _____

Account No _____

Please pay Royal Bank of Scotland plc, London Drummonds Branch, 49 Charing Cross, London SW1A 2DX (Sort Code 16-00-38), for the account of BRF A/C No. 00774151

The sum of _____ pounds on ___ /___ /___ (insert date your standing order starts) and thereafter the same amount on the same day of each month until further notice.

Signature _____ Date _____

Single donation

☐ I enclose my cheque/credit card/Switch card details for a donation of

£5 £10 £25 £50 £100 £250 (other) £ _____ to support BRF's ministry

Credit/ Switch card no. ☐☐☐☐☐☐☐☐☐☐☐☐☐☐☐☐☐☐☐

Expires ☐☐ ☐☐   Issue no. of Switch card ☐☐☐

Signature _____ Date _____

(Where appropriate, on receipt of your donation, we will send you a Gift Aid form)

☐ **Please send me information about making a bequest to BRF in my will.**

Please detach and send this completed form to: Richard Fisher, BRF,
15 The Chambers, Vineyard, Abingdon OX14 3FE. BRF is a Registered Charity (No.233280)

ND0209

BIBLE READING RESOURCES (updated and expanded)

An updated pack of resources and ideas to help to promote Bible reading in your church is available from BRF. The pack, which will be of use at any time during the year (but especially for Bible Sunday in October), includes sample readings from BRF's Bible reading notes and *The People's Bible Commentary*, a sermon outline, an all-age sketch, a children's activity, information about BRF's ministry and much more.

Unless you specify the month in which you would like the pack sent, we will send it immediately on receipt of your order. We greatly appreciate your donations towards the cost of producing the pack (without them we would not be able to make the pack available) and we welcome your comments about the contents of the pack and your ideas for future ones.

This coupon should be sent to:

BRF
15 The Chambers
Vineyard
Abingdon
OX14 3FE

Name _____

Address _____

_____ Postcode _____

Telephone _____

Email _____

Please send me _____ Bible Reading Resources Pack(s)

Please send the pack now/ in _____ (month).

I enclose a donation for £ _____ towards the cost of the pack.

BRF is a Registered Charity

❏ Please send me a Bible reading resources pack to encourage Bible reading in my church

❏ I would like to take out a subscription myself (complete your name and address details only once)

❏ I would like to give a gift subscription (please complete both name and address sections below)

Your name _____

Your address _____

_____ Postcode _____

Gift subscription name _____

Gift subscription address _____

_____ Postcode _____

Please send *New Daylight* beginning with the September 2009 / January 2010 issue: (delete as applicable)

(please tick box)	UK	SURFACE	AIR MAIL
NEW DAYLIGHT	❏ £13.80	❏ £15.00	❏ £17.10
NEW DAYLIGHT 3-year sub	❏ £33.00		
NEW DAYLIGHT DELUXE	❏ £17.40	❏ £21.90	❏ £27.00

I would like to take out an annual subscription to *Quiet Spaces* beginning with the next available issue:

(please tick box)	UK	SURFACE	AIR MAIL
QUIET SPACES	❏ £16.95	❏ £18.45	❏ £20.85

Please complete the payment details below and send your coupon, with appropriate payment, to:
BRF, 15 The Chambers, Vineyard, Abingdon OX14 3FE.

Total enclosed £ _____ (cheques should be made payable to 'BRF')

Payment by cheque ❏ postal order ❏ Visa ❏ Mastercard ❏ Switch ❏

Card number:

Expires: ☐☐☐☐   Security code ☐☐☐   Issue no (Switch): ☐☐☐☐

Signature (essential if paying by credit/Switch card) _____

BRF is a Registered Charity

BRF PUBLICATIONS ORDER FORM

Please ensure that you complete and send off both sides of this order form.
Please send me the following book(s):

		Quantity	Price	Total
612 2	Good Enough Mother (N. Starkey)	_____	£5.99	_____
587 3	Into Your Hands (K. Scully)	_____	£5.99	_____
687 0	My First Communion (A.M. Burrin)	_____	£5.99	_____
682 5	A Child's Book of Saints (C. Doyle)	_____	£6.99	_____
610 8	Bible Reading—a Beginner's Guide (M. Green)	_____	£4.99	_____
503 3	Messy Church (L. Moore)	_____	£8.99	_____
602 3	Messy Church 2 (L. Moore)	_____	£8.99	_____
461 6	The Growth of Love (K.J. White)	_____	£8.99	_____
386 2	From the Ground Up (K. Copsey)	_____	£6.99	_____
464 7	Footsteps to the Feast (M. Payne)	_____	£8.99	_____
218 6	The Challenge of Cell Church (P. Potter)	_____	£7.99	_____
604 7	The Challenge of Change (P. Potter)	_____	£7.99	_____
615 3	How Would Jesus Lead Worship? (S. & S. Hargreaves)	_____	£6.99	_____
066 3	PBC: Exodus (H.R. Page Jr)	_____	£8.99	_____
030 4	PBC: 1 & 2 Samuel (H. Mowvley)	_____	£7.99	_____
046 5	PBC: Mark (D. France)	_____	£8.99	_____
122 6	PBC: 1 Corinthians (J. Murphy-O'Connor)	_____	£7.99	_____

Total cost of books £ _____
Donation £ _____
Postage and packing £ _____
TOTAL £ _____

POSTAGE AND PACKING CHARGES

order value	UK	Europe	Surface	Air Mail
£7.00 & under	£1.25	£3.00	£3.50	£5.50
£7.01–£30.00	£2.25	£5.50	£6.50	£10.00
Over £30.00	free	prices on request		

See over for payment details. All prices are correct at time of going to press, are subject to the prevailing rate of VAT and may be subject to change without prior warning.

PAYMENT DETAILS

Please complete the payment details below and send with appropriate payment and completed order form to:

**BRF, 15 The Chambers, Vineyard,
Abingdon OX14 3FE**

Name _____

Address _____

_____

_____ Postcode _____

Telephone _____

Email _____

Total enclosed £ _____(cheques should be made payable to 'BRF')

Payment by cheque ❏ postal order ❏ Visa ❏ Mastercard ❏ Switch ❏

Card number: | | | | | | | | | | | | | | | | | | |

Expires: | | | | Security code | | | Issue no (Switch only): | | | |

Signature (essential if paying by credit/Switch card) _____

❏ Please do not send me further information about BRF publications.

ALTERNATIVE WAYS TO ORDER

Christian bookshops: All good Christian bookshops stock BRF publications. For your nearest stockist, please contact BRF.

Telephone: The BRF office is open between 09.15 and 17.30.
To place your order, phone 01865 319700; fax 01865 319701.

Web: Visit www.brf.org.uk

BRF is a Registered Charity

Subscribe today to *New Daylight*

and ensure you get your copy in good time for the start of the next issue!

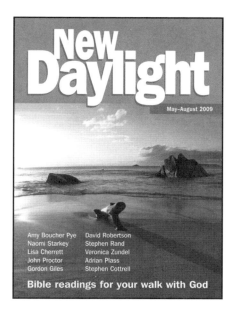

With each issue of *New Daylight*, you also receive:

- **BRF News**: keep in touch with what is happening at BRF
- **BRF Prayer Diary**: a chance to pray for specific events and people in our organization
- **Information** about BRF's new books, Quiet Days and resources

SUBSCRIPTIONS

❑ I would like to take out a subscription myself (complete your name and address details only once)

❑ I would like to give a gift subscription (please complete both name and address sections below)

Your name _____

Your address _____

_____ Postcode _____

Tel. no _____ Email address: _____

Gift subscription name _____

Gift subscription address _____

_____ Postcode _____

Please send *New Daylight* beginning with the September 2009 / January 2010 issue: (delete as applicable)

(please tick box)	UK	SURFACE	AIR MAIL
NEW DAYLIGHT	❑ £13.80	❑ £15.00	❑ £17.10
NEW DAYLIGHT 3-year sub	❑ £33.00		
NEW DAYLIGHT DELUXE	❑ £17.40	❑ £21.90	❑ £27.00

Total enclosed £ _____ (cheques made payable to 'BRF')

Payment: cheque ❑ postal order ❑ Visa ❑ Mastercard ❑ Switch ❑

Card no: ☐☐☐☐☐☐☐☐☐☐☐☐☐☐☐☐☐☐

Expires ☐☐☐☐ Security code ☐☐☐ Issue no (Switch) ☐☐☐☐

Signature (essential if paying by credit/Switch card):

_____

Please complete the details above and return the card, along with appropriate payment, to:

Subscriptions, BRF, 15 The Chambers, Vineyard, Abingdon OX14 3FE.

BRF is a Registered Charity

ND0209